dream
machines
motorcycles

dream
machines
motorcycles

roland brown

p

Above: Honda's CB750 four of 1969 is regarded as the first 'superbike', and was arguably the most significant and influential motorcycle of the 20th century.

Opposite: BSA's racy 500cc single-cylinder Gold Star DBD34 was one of the machines that helped British manufacturers dominate the motorcycle scene in the 1950s.

This is a Parragon Book

First published in 2002

Parragon
Queen Street House
4 Queen Street
Bath BA1 1HE, UK

Copyright © Parragon 2002

Designed, produced and packaged by
Stonecastle Graphics Limited

Text by Roland Brown
Edited by Philip de Ste. Croix
Designed by Paul Turner and Sue Pressley

ISBN 0-75257-458-2

Printed in China

Photographic credits:

(l) = left, (c) = centre, (r) = right, (t) = top, (b) = below.

Ray Archer/R Brown: page 85*(t)*.
© Roland Brown: pages 1, 4, 21*(t)*, 33, 34, 36*(b)*, 37, 40, 41*(b)*, 44, 45*(tl)*, 50*(b)*, 51, 54-55, 56, 57*(t)*, 72, 73*(t)*, 74, 75*(cr)*, 76, 77*(c)*, 78-79, 80*(b)*, 81, 84, 85*(b)*, 91*(t)*, 95*(tr)*, 95*(cl)*.
Paul Bryant/R Brown: page 77*(t)*, 77*(b)*.
Jack Burnicle (© Roland Brown): pages 38*(t)*, 48, 49*(l)*.
Jason Critchell/R Brown: pages 90, 91*(c)*, 91*(b)*.
Patrick Curtet/R Brown: page 80*(t)*.
Richard Francis/R Brown: page 70*(t)*.
Gold & Goose (© Roland Brown): pages 29*(cr)*, 31*(br)*, 75*(bl)*.
© Gold & Goose: pages 60-61, 64, 65*(l)*, 68-69, 70*(b)*, 71.
© Patrick Gosling (© Roland Brown): pages 15*(r)*, 39*(br)*.
Phil Masters (© Roland Brown): pages 2, 5, 7*(t)*, 20, 21*(bl)*, 21*(br)*, 22-23, 24-25, 32*(t)*, 41*(t)*, 42-43, 46-47, 49*(r)*, 57*(b)*, 66-67, 73*(b)*, 75*(t)*, 82-83, 86-87, 88-89, 92-93.
© Andrew Morland: pages 8-9, 12, 13*(b)*, 14, 15*(l)*, 16-17, 18-19, 26, 27*(t)*, 27*(c)*, 30*(b)*, 31*(bl)*, 38*(b)*, 39*(bl)*.
© Don Morley: pages 58-59.
© Colin Schiller: page 63*(tl)*, 63*(b)*.
© Garry Stuart: pages 3, 10-11, 13*(t)*, 27*(b)*, 30*(cr)*, 32*(b)*, 35.
Oli Tennent (© Roland Brown): pages 6, 7*(b)*, 28, 29*(tl)*, 29*(b)*, 36*(t)*, 45*(tr)*, 45*(b)*, 50*(t)*, 52-53, 62, 63*(tr)*, 65*(r)*, 94, 95*(b)*.

Contents

Introduction

The evolution of the motorcycle from the simple motorized bicycles of the late 19th century to the sophisticated, multi-cylinder superbikes of the present day is a fascinating journey. Along the way there have been many outstanding machines; bikes famed for their performance, technical brilliance or good looks – and often for all three qualities…and more!

There's a revealing symmetry about the fact that this collection of motorcycling's finest should start and finish with Harley-Davidson. Both the early Model 11F and the latest VRSCA V-Rod are powered by a large-capacity V-twin engine. The fact that the 11F produces 10bhp and has a top speed of 60mph (97km/h) and the V-Rod makes more than 10 times as much power and is capable of 140mph (225km/h) highlights the huge advances that have been made in the intervening years.

The V-Rod is not particularly fast by modern superbike standards, though it undoubtedly qualifies for any book with the title *Dream Machines* by virtue of its sheer desirability and style. Other bikes, too, such as the sophisticated Ariel Square Four and glamorous Indian Chief earn their inclusion because of qualities other than sheer speed.

But over the years it has tended to be the fastest bikes that have provided the most excitement and technical interest, and there are no apologies for leaning the *Dream Machines* guest list in their favour. Especially when the result is such a glittering and accomplished line-up of machinery that not only includes the greatest two-wheeled names but also traces the story of motorcycling over more than a century of development.

The layout of the motorcycle as we know it took some time to become established. The first ever bike, Gottlieb Daimler's Einspur ('One-track') of 1885, was a cumbersome wooden contraption powered by a 265cc single-cylinder four-stroke engine. Nine years later, also in Germany,

Below: Harley's V-Rod is powered by a big V-twin engine, just like its Model 11 predecessor of more than 80 years earlier – but that's where the similarity ends. This is the author warming the rear tyre before launching the 115bhp machine down the Irwindale drag strip, near Los Angeles, during the V-Rod's press introduction in June 2001.

Left: Ariel's Square Four was one of the most glamorous bikes on the road during a production run that lasted, with numerous updates, for almost 30 years.

Below: Indian's Chief had already been in production for almost two decades when the Springfield firm introduced its famous skirted fenders in 1940. Production ended finally in 1953, but the Indian name and image remains strong and has resulted in a recent rebirth.

Hildebrand and Wolfmüller's first ever production motorcycle had a liquid-cooled, 1500cc twin-cylinder engine in a specially made steel frame, and also featured pneumatic tyres – a recent invention. It was good for 25mph (40km/h), which doubtless felt fast given the fact that the rear brake was merely a metal bar that dragged on the ground.

Another important advance came soon afterwards from France, when Count Albert de Dion and Georges Bouton combined to created a compact and reliable four-stroke single-cylinder engine of about 125cc. The De Dion Bouton was widely copied and used in a wide variety of three- and two-wheeled machines. But the motorcycle as we know it first appeared in 1901 when another French duo, the Werner brothers, moved their bike's motor from above the front wheel to between the wheels, in a triangulated frame.

The so-called 'New Werner', whose layout gave improved handling due to its low centre of gravity, also featured a bicycle-style saddle, wheel-rim brakes and final drive by a leather belt. Also in 1901, in the United States, George Hendee and Oscar Hedstrom combined to produce the first Indian; shortly afterwards Harley-Davidson in Milwaukee built its first bike. By the end of the decade, a large and growing number of firms in both America and Europe were producing machines exhibiting a variety of styles and engine layouts. The motorcycle had truly arrived – and our story was just beginning.

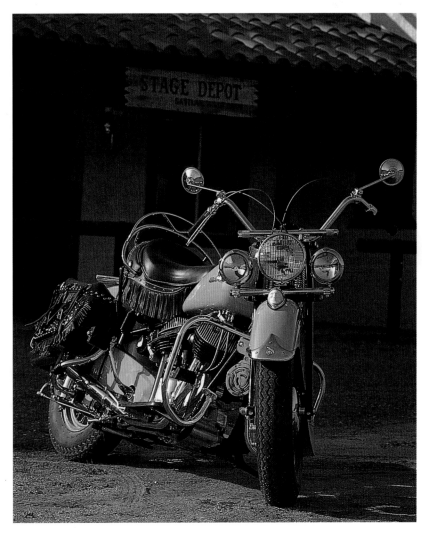

Harley-Davidson Model 11F

**Top speed
60mph**
97km/h

*Right: Like several other
American manufacturers in
motorcycling's early years,
Harley-Davidson decided
that two single-cylinder
engines would make a
useful twin, especially if set
at 45 degrees apart.*

*Below: The Model 11F's
performance was often
exciting, especially given
the fact that the bike had no
front brake and only a crude
expanding band system on
the rear wheel.*

 The Model 11F of 1915 proved that
Harley-Davidson's founders learned fast
when it came to building V-twin
motorbikes. The 11F was a good-looking, efficient
and deservedly popular machine. Its 989cc V-twin
engine produced about 10bhp, good for a top speed
of about 60mph (97km/h), and the bike came with
up-to-date features including footboards and chain
final drive.

Yet the Milwaukee firm's founders, William
Harley and the three Davidson brothers (Arthur,
Walter and William), had suffered a serious setback
six years earlier when, encouraged by the success
of their pioneering single-cylinder models, they had
introduced their first V-twin. The Model 5D of
1909 had an 811cc engine, with cylinders set at the
45-degree angle that would become a Harley
trademark. It produced about 7hp, twice as much as
the firm's single. But the 5D was hard to start,
suffered from technical problems including a
slipping drive belt, and was promptly withdrawn
from the market.

This did not deter William Harley and the
Davidsons, whose robust single-cylinder models
were increasingly in demand. The quartet had
founded the firm in 1903, in a small shed in the
Davidsons' yard. Their early single became known
as the Silent Grey Fellow, due to its colour and

efficient exhaust muffler. Production rose dramatically, from just 49 bikes in 1906 to more than 3000 in 1910 – by which time the firm had moved to larger premises in what would become Juneau Avenue, still the current address.

The next year, Harley-Davidson reintroduced the V-twin as the Model 7D. (H-D regarded 1904 as year zero, so 1911 was the seventh model year.) It featured an improved valve system, still with the original inlet-over-exhaust layout, plus a tensioner for the drive belt. It also had a new, stronger frame. This was a much improved bike, but William Harley, the firm's chief engineer, did not rest on his laurels. During the next few years he introduced a host of improvements that established Harley-Davidson as one of America's leading manufacturers.

'Ful Floteing' system

For 1912 the V-twin was made available with a larger 989cc engine, developing 8bhp, and could be ordered with the option of a clutch (in the rear wheel hub), and with chain instead of belt final drive. Further improvements included a more sophisticated lubrication system, a new frame that gave a lower seat, and a sprung seat post – the curiously named 'Ful Floteing' system – for added comfort. Two years later came more advances: footboards, enclosed valve springs, a kick-starter and two-speed transmission.

By 1915, when the Model 11F was introduced, Harley had established a V-twin format that would hold the firm in good stead for the next 15 years. Although other refinements would soon be added,

notably with the three-speed Model J, Harley had produced a big V-twin whose performance and strength would win many admirers, until it was replaced by the side-valve V Series in 1930.

For Harley, 1915 was memorable for another reason too: the firm's first competition success. After initial resistance to racing at the Milwaukee factory, ex-racer Bill Ottaway had been hired to run a factory team, and had developed a tuned and lightened version of the V-twin, the 11K. After breakdowns in its first season, the 100mph (161km/h) 11K took its rider Otto Walker to victory, against factory opposition, in two prestigious 300-mile (483km) races. Harley's hard-riding 'Wrecking Crew' would have many more wins in the years to come, many of them on powerful, purpose-built, eight-valve V-twins.

Below: The 11F's two-speed gearbox was operated by hand using a lever to the left of the tank. Another job for the rider was to lubricate the motor using a hand-operated oil pump.

Bottom left: Although some rival firms including Indian offered a basic form of rear suspension, Harley stuck to a 'hard-tail' frame, and improved the rider's comfort with a sprung saddle and 'Ful Floteing' seat post design.

Specification	Harley-Davidson Model 11F (1915)
Engine	Air-cooled four-valve inlet-over-exhaust 45-degree V-twin
Capacity	989cc (84 x 88.9mm)
Maximum power	10bhp
Transmission	Two-speed, chain or belt final drive
Frame	Steel single downtube
Suspension	Girder forks; rigid rear
Brakes	None front; expanding band rear
Weight	310lb (141kg)
Top speed	60mph (97km/h)

Indian Powerplus

**Top speed
65mph**
105km/h

Indian was the biggest American manufacturer in motorcycling's early years, producing large numbers of V-twins from its sprawling factory, known as the Wigwam, in Springfield, Massachusetts. Indians were fast, in every sense. They won races on board tracks, dirt tracks and even at the Isle of Man TT (where Indian took first, second and third in 1911). They set top speed records and posted quickest ever times for coast-to-coast trips across America.

Among the best and most influential of the early Indians was the Powerplus, which was introduced in 1916. As its name suggested, its engine was a more powerful version of Indian's existing unit, a 42-degree V-twin. The Powerplus had a side-valve layout in place of the traditional F-head (or inlet-over-exhaust) design that had been Indian's mainstay since the firm's first twin-cylinder model of 1907.

Ironically, Indian's best days were already in the past when the Powerplus arrived. The firm had been set up in 1901 by George Hendee and Oscar Hedstrom, two former bicycle racers, and had grown quickly. Production reached almost 5000

bikes in 1909, and by 1913 was over 32,000. But the following year Henry Ford set up his first car assembly line, and the US motorcycle market took a sharp downturn. Indian would never sell as many bikes again.

Co-founder and chief engineer Oscar Hedstrom retired in 1913. The Powerplus was designed by Charles Gustafson Snr., who had previously worked for Reading Standard, which had built America's first side-valve bikes. The new machine met with resistance from some Indian owners loyal to Hedstrom's F-head machines. But one ride normally won them over, because the Powerplus lived up to its name by delivering considerable extra performance.

Its 998cc long-stroke engine produced a claimed 18bhp, well up on the previous Big Twin, and gave the Powerplus a top speed of over 60mph (97km/h). The new motor was also cleaner and quieter, due to its enclosed valvegear. It had a three-speed gearbox with a hand change and foot clutch. There was also a back-up hand clutch lever, located to the right of the fuel tank because Indian's throttle was on the left.

Below: Finished in Indian's traditional maroon, the Powerplus lived up to its name by delivering plenty of performance with its 18bhp, 42-degree side-valve V-twin engine. Long-distance ace Cannonball Baker's string of high-speed record runs helped make the model popular, and it remained in production for almost a decade with few changes.

The Powerplus chassis was similar to that of the old model – understandably, because Indian was already offering optional leaf-spring rear suspension, years before most manufacturers would do so. A leaf-spring design was also used for the front suspension. Controls were via a complex system of rods and linkages until 1918, when cables were introduced.

Record-breaking performance

Long-distance legend Erwin 'Cannonball' Baker gave the Powerplus the perfect introduction in late 1915, when he used a pre-production bike to set a new Canada-to-Mexico Three Flags record – covering the 1655.5 miles (2664.2km) in 3 days, 9 hours and 15 minutes. The following year, he set a 24-hour record of 1018.7 miles (1639.4km) in Australia, despite hazards including giant parakeets and driving rain. And in 1917, Baker rode a

Specification	Indian Powerplus (1918)
Engine	Air-cooled four-valve side-valve 42-degree V-twin
Capacity	998cc (79.4 x 100.8mm)
Maximum power	18bhp
Transmission	Three-speed, chain final drive
Frame	Steel single downtube
Suspension	Leaf-spring front and (optional) rear
Brakes	None front; drum rear
Weight	410lb (186kg)
Top speed	65mph (105km/h)

Powerplus to another 24-hour record of 1534.7 miles (2469.8km) on the Cincinnati board track.

The Powerplus itself also proved impressively long-lasting, remaining in production until 1924 with few changes. It did, however, gain a new name in its old age. Following the Chief's introduction in 1922, the Powerplus was restyled the Standard to avoid overshadowing the new model.

Below left: Indian's left-hand throttle control meant that levers for compression release and gearshift, along with the back-up clutch operation, were located on the right side of the Powerplus fuel tank.

Indian's Eight-valve Heroes

Indian gained considerable publicity from the exploits of its racers, notably the daring board-track stars including Jake de Rosier, Charles 'Fearless' Balke and Eddie Hasha. They rode tuned, stripped-down V-twins which diced at well over 100mph (161km/h) on the steep boards. But the sport went into decline following the deaths of Hasha, Johnnie Albright another Indian pilot and six spectators at a New Jersey track in 1912. De Rosier, winner of over 900 races and the holder of many speed records, left Indian for Excelsior. He died of racing injuries in 1913.

Above: Indian's board-race bikes were powered by fire-breathing eight-valve V-twin engines with open exhausts. Low handlebars gave racers a streamlined riding position.

Left: This bike's leaf-spring rear suspension was a factory optional extra. Indian's leaf-spring front suspension system was used for racing and hillclimb bikes, as well as roadsters.

Brough Superior

**Top speed
100mph**
161km/h

*Below: This 1932-model
SS100 was owned by
George Brough's most
famous customer, Lawrence
of Arabia. After Lawrence's
first ride, he wrote to
Brough: 'It is the silkiest
thing I have ever ridden...
I think this is going to be a
very excellent bike... I am
very grateful to you and
everybody for the care
taken to make her perfect.'*

There is not much doubt about which was the fastest and most glamorous of pre-Second World War roadsters. The Brough Superior SS100 was a big, handsome, high-performance V-twin which, in the words of its creator, George Brough, was 'made up to an ideal and not down to a price'. Fewer than 400 examples of the SS100 were built between 1925 and 1940. For most of that time, there was nothing on two wheels that could match it.

George Brough was a master publicist. He summed up the SS100's appeal when he wrote in a 1926 catalogue that it 'is a machine made essentially for an experienced motorcyclist who realises that just as a racehorse needs more attention than a hunter, so an SS100, with its colossal output of power, requires more attention than the average sports machine. Give it the necessary attention and you have a machine that can always be relied upon to show its back number plate to anything on wheels likely to be met on the roads.'

Signed guarantee

Brough, the son of a motorcycle manufacturer, assembled his bikes with the assistance of a small team of enthusiasts at a workshop in Haydn Road, Nottingham. He called his first big twin the SS80, after its top speed of 80mph (129km/h). The SS100 was the logical and even faster follow-up, and was delivered with a signed guarantee that the machine had been timed at over 100mph (161km/h) for a quarter of a mile.

The precise specification of Brough's bikes varied considerably, with even the engine of the SS100 being changed over the years. Initial models used a 988cc JAP V-twin unit that produced over 40bhp; the final 100 machines were powered by a similar-capacity V-twin from AMC (Matchless). What did not change was George Brough's refusal to accept anything less than the best. Manufacturers including JAP-built 'Special for Brough' parts; many components were returned to their makers to be redesigned and improved.

Hard-riding Brough and his fellow Superior riders, including notables such as Freddie Dixon, Eric Fernihough and Bert Le Vack, took the Nottingham-built machines to a string of victories in races, hillclimbs and sprints. This fuelled Brough's talent for publicity, which had revealed itself when he had coined the name Superior, prompting his father's reply: 'I suppose that makes mine the Inferior?'

'The Rolls-Royce of Motorcycles'
Brough's SS100 brochure promised 'hands-off stability at 95mph' (153km/h), but it was George's slogan 'The Rolls-Royce of Motorcycles' that made most impact. Adapted from a line in a magazine test of a Brough, the phrase initially displeased bosses at the luxury car firm. But after a Rolls executive had arrived at Haydn Road to find Brough workers wearing white gloves – to avoid marking the show bikes they were assembling – all objections were dropped.

The most famous Superior enthusiast was T.E. Lawrence (Lawrence of Arabia), who owned a special stainless steel petrol tank which he fitted to his series of Broughs. Lawrence wrote of his love of high-speed travel aboard his Superiors, but he died after a crash while riding one, probably following a collision with a cyclist.

George Brough was never content with the SS100's performance, and produced various special models, notably the Alpine Grand Sports, which was intended for rapid touring. Fastest of all was the legendary SS100 Pendine, named after the long beach in south Wales where many speed records were set. With its low bars, rearset footrests and high-compression engine, the Pendine was good for a genuine 110mph (177km/h). Brough production stopped when the Second World War began, and did not restart afterwards.

Left: Lawrence's SS100 is powered by a 998cc V-twin engine from JAP of north London. A horizontal spring of the Bentley and Draper rear suspension system is visible below the saddle. The system worked well but required regular maintenance of bushes to ensure good handling.

Specification	Brough Superior SS100 (1925)
Engine	Air-cooled ohv four-valve pushrod 50-degree V-twin
Capacity	988cc (85.5 x 86mm)
Maximum power	45bhp @ 5000rpm
Transmission	Four-speed, chain final drive
Frame	Steel single downtube
Suspension	Girder forks; twin springs rear
Brakes	Drum front and rear
Weight	396lb (180kg)
Top speed	100mph (161km/h)

Norton International

**Top speed
90mph**
145km/h

*Right: The CS1, predecessor
of the International, became
an instant hit when it took
the race win and lap record
at the 1937 Senior TT.*

*Below: Similar silver and
black Norton paintwork for
the International, easily
distinguishable because its
exhaust pipe is on the right
instead of the left.*

Norton established such a mighty
reputation in motorcycling's early years,
most notably with a string of Isle of Man
TT victories, that when the Birmingham firm added
the prefix 'Unapproachable' to its name in its
advertising, few people complained. That
reputation began with the early singles and twins
that had side-valve or pushrod-operated overhead-
valve engine layouts. But it was Norton's later pair
of overhead-cam singles, the CS1 and especially
the International, that made the biggest impact.

The CS1 (short for Cam Shaft 1) was much
needed when it was introduced in 1927, because
Norton's future did not look bright. Founder James
Lansdowne 'Pa' Norton had died two years earlier,
aged 56, following a history of heart problems.
There had been no Isle of Man victory that year,
and only the riding ability of new star Stanley
Woods had earned a win in the Senior TT in 1926.
The days of Norton's pushrod single seemed
numbered and a replacement was needed.

Blaze of glory

Enter Walter Moore, Norton's race team manager
and development engineer, who redesigned the
pushrod engine with overhead-camshaft valvegear
to create the CS1. Moore did the design work for
the 'cammy' engine at home, before offering it to
Norton. The 490cc unit featured a vertical camshaft
tower, and traditional long-stroke dimensions of 79

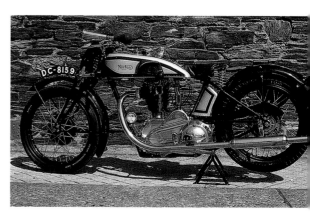

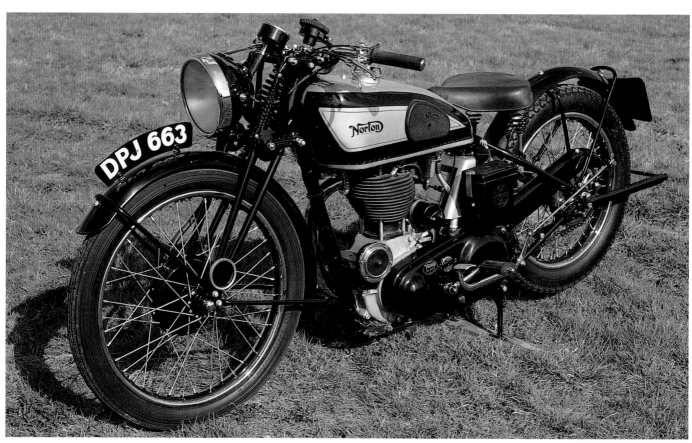

Racing Single – The Mighty Manx

Norton's dominance of Isle of Man TT racing in the 1930s led to the racing version of the International being christened the Manx. The single was updated many times, notably in 1937 with a dohc valve design. In 1950, Irish brothers Rex and Cromie McCandless produced an innovative tubular steel frame, the Featherbed. It gained this name because of racer Harold Daniell's comment that riding the new bike was like sitting on a feather bed. Geoff Duke won 500 and 350cc world championships on the Manx in 1951, retaining the 350 title in '52. Although the single was eventually outgunned by more powerful Italian fours, a Manx ridden by Godfrey Nash won the Yugoslavian GP in 1969.

Specification	Norton International (1932)
Engine	Air-cooled sohc two-valve single
Capacity	490cc (79 x 100mm)
Maximum power	29bhp @ 5500rpm
Transmission	Four-speed, chain final drive
Frame	Steel cradle
Suspension	Girder front; rigid rear
Brakes	Drum front and rear
Weight	355lb (161kg)
Top speed (road trim)	90mph (145km/h)

x 100mm. The CS1 arrived in a blaze of glory when Alec Bennett won the 1937 Senior TT, with Woods breaking the lap record on a similar bike.

Norton was back, and in the following year the CS1 was made available as a super-sports roadster. But the next two seasons were disappointing for the team from Norton's Bracebridge Street factory, made worse when Moore accepted a lucrative offer from German firm NSU – and took his engine design with him. NSU's subsequent 500SS was so similar to the CS1 that Norton workers joked that the initials stood for Norton Spares Used.

Norton needed a new engine, and got one in 1931 when Arthur Carroll redesigned the CS1, under the direction of race boss Joe Craig. Carroll's design had identical cylinder dimensions, but the camshaft drive was new, and the exhaust pipe exited on the right instead of the left. The new engine's 30bhp output gave a top speed of over 100mph (161km/h) in racing trim, and triggered great success for Norton, whose works team dominated the Continental grands prix and took first, second and third in the Senior TT.

Norton produced a similar model for sale in 1932, calling it the International in recognition of the previous season's success. Customers could opt for road or track specification, and initially there were few differences, apart from a silencer that reduced top speed to about 90mph (145km/h). The Inter's impressive specification included Amal TT carburettor, four-speed gearbox, and Webb competition girder forks. The model remained popular throughout the 1930s, and survived in various forms well into the 1950s.

Above left: Arthur Carroll's second-generation 'cammy' single-cylinder engine shared the CS1's dimensions of 79 x 100mm but, as well as its right-sided exhaust pipe, had a redesigned camshaft bevel-drive system.

Harley-Davidson Knucklehead

**Top speed
100mph**
161km/h

*Below: The basic shape of
the Model EL was very
similar to that of the
uprated, side-valve Model
VLH that was also
introduced in 1936, but
there was no doubt about
which bike was the faster
and more important. This
V-twin's shiny rocker-box
covers confirmed that this
was the firm's long-awaited
overhead-valve powerplant.*

Many Harley enthusiasts would argue that the Model 61E, nicknamed the Knucklehead, was the most important bike that the Motor Compnay has ever introduced. It was certainly one of the bravest. When the Knucklehead – so called after the shape of its rocker boxes – was being developed in the mid-1930s, America was struggling through the Depression. Businesses were closing, wages were being cut, bike sales were poor.

Yet after some debate, Harley – whose range had a reputation for reliability but not performance – went ahead with the new machine, which was introduced in 1936. The Model E's 45-degree V-twin engine had a capacity of 989cc (or 61 cubic inches, hence that part of its name), and was notable for two main reasons. The first was its lubrication system, which re-circulated the oil to a reservoir tank, instead of the relatively crude total-loss system used before.

Secondly, the Model E was Harley's first production bike with overhead valves, instead of the less efficient side-valves. This – at last! – meant extra power. A maximum of 37bhp for the basic Model 61E, with its 6.5:1 compression ratio, and an impressive 40bhp for the 61EL, which had 7:1 compression and was good for a genuine 100mph (161km/h) on the open road.

The twin-cradle steel frame was also new (it had also been designed to suit the large-capacity side-valve Model V), and held an improved version of Harley's springer front suspension system. Other features included a four-speed gearbox and a new fuel tank, which wore classical art-deco emblems as well as holding Harley's first standard-fitment speedometer in a console on its top.

The 61E was a very stylish motorcycle, with a purposeful, muscular look enhanced by the way the new oil tank filled the space between the V-twin engine and the rear fender. And although the bike

suffered from numerous teething problems – notably with oil leaks and the frame's inability to cope with the engine's power – the Knucklehead quickly captured American motorcyclists' imagination.

What made Milwaukee famous...

It was Harley's good luck – or, perhaps, a reward for earlier bravery – that the Depression was easing by the time the 61E reached the market in 1936. Almost 2000 units were built and sold in the first year, ahead of target. Even more importantly, the Knucklehead's design and performance gave Harley an edge over great rival Indian for the first time in years – an advantage that Milwaukee would never surrender.

Just to confirm the new model's performance potential, in March 1937 Harley sent racer Joe Petrali to Daytona Beach with a tuned Knucklehead modified for improved aerodynamics with a small fairing, disc front wheel and an all-enveloping tail section. Over a measured mile, Petrali roared to a two-way average speed of 136.183mph (219.2km/h), setting a new record and generating plenty of publicity in the process.

Back in 1937, not even Harley could have imagined that the Knucklehead's basic engine layout would serve the company into the 21st century. But after the first major overhaul, with the 1213cc Model 74F in 1941, the firm has repeatedly

Specification	Harley-Davidson Model 61EL (1936)
Engine	Air-cooled ohv four-valve pushrod 45-degree V-twin
Capacity	989cc (84 x 88.9mm)
Maximum power	40bhp @ 4800rpm
Transmission	Four-speed, chain final drive
Frame	Steel twin downtube
Suspension	Springer forks; rigid rear
Brakes	Drum front and rear
Weight	515lb (234kg)
Top speed	100mph (161km/h)

updated its big V-twin engine, without changing its essential design. And despite the recent arrival of more modern powerplants from Milwaukee, the faithful air-cooled, pushrod-operated, ohv 45-degree V-twin shows no sign of being abandoned just yet.

Left: Looking at those rocker-box covers, it's easy to understand why the Model E acquired the nickname Knucklehead. Harley's stylish fuel tank emblem was used between 1936 and 1939.

Below: The Model E had a new frame as well as its new engine, but there was still no sign of a rear suspension system. The four-speed gearbox was operated by a lever to the left of the fuel tank.

Triumph Speed Twin

**Top speed
93mph**
150km/h

Below: Edward Turner was a fine stylist as well as an engineer, and the Speed Twin had the looks to match its parallel-twin engine's performance. Early models such as this had girder front forks and rigid rear end; later Twins combined similar maroon and chrome finish with telescopic forks and plunger rear suspension.

 Motorcycling was changed for ever when the Speed Twin burst onto the scene in 1937, dramatically proving that two cylinders could be better than one, and triggering an era of parallel twin dominance that would last for more than three decades. It's doubtful whether any British bike has had more influence on those that followed.

The Speed Twin's appeal was easy to understand. Triumph boss Edward Turner's 498cc masterpiece was fast, stylish, practical and reasonably priced, with a distinct performance advantage over the majority of single-cylinder machines that had dominated motorcycle production until then. Turner himself, rarely reluctant to express an opinion, was in no doubt about a twin's attributes.

'A twin gives better torque,' he said. 'It will run at higher revolutions than a single of similar capacity without unduly stressing major components. Because the firing intervals are equal, which means even torque, the low-speed pulling is better. The engine gives faster acceleration, is more durable, is easier to silence and is better cooled. In every way it is a more agreeable engine to handle.'

Effortless cruising

Most riders found it hard to disagree after riding the Speed Twin, which was matched by some singles in its top speed of just over 90mph (145km/h), but not in the relatively smooth and effortless way it would cruise at more than 70mph (113km/h). The pushrod-operated engine, which had a 360-degree firing arrangement (pistons rising and falling together), was quite softly tuned, with a 7:1 compression ratio and a maximum output of 29bhp at 6000rpm. Although there was some vibration, by single standards it was smooth.

Turner had recently arrived from Ariel (where he had designed the Square Four), after that firm had taken over Triumph. He had announced himself by revamping Triumph's range of 500, 350 and 250cc singles, boosting sales with fresh styling and catchy new names: Tiger 90, 80 and 70. Turner's rare talent for both marketing and styling were again evident in the Speed Twin, with its evocative name and handsome lines.

Handling rated highly

The Twin's lean, simple look was not misleading. It used essentially the same frame and forks as the Tiger 90, was actually slightly lighter than the 500 single, and its engine was slightly narrower. The drum brakes were powerful and handling was rated highly, although the rigid rear end tended to hop over bumps.

It was the engine, though, that sent the testers of the day into rapture. 'On the open road the machine was utterly delightful,' reported *The Motor Cycle*. 'Ample power was always available at a turn of the twist-grip, and the lack of noise when the machine was cruising in the seventies was almost uncanny.' The magazine managed a two-way average of 93.7mph (151km/h) and a 'truly amazing' one-way best of 107mph (172km/h).

Predictably, given all this and the Triumph's competitive price of little more than the Tiger 90, the bike was a huge success. The outbreak of the Second World War put a halt to development, but by 1948, three year's after war's end, all the main manufacturers had parallel twins of their own. Meanwhile the Speed Twin had been tuned to create a sports model, the Tiger 100, and a 650cc derivative was also being developed. Triumph's parallel twin revolution was well under way.

Above left: A fuel tank insert containing dials was a typical Triumph feature of the 1930s.

Above: Triumph's powerful and relatively smooth 498cc engine triggered the British bike industry's adoption of the parallel twin layout.

Specification	Triumph Speed Twin (1938)
Engine	Air-cooled ohv four-valve pushrod parallel twin
Capacity	498cc (63 x 80mm)
Maximum power	29bhp @ 6000rpm
Transmission	Four-speed, chain final drive
Frame	Steel twin downtube
Suspension	Girder front; rigid rear
Brakes	Drum front and rear
Weight	365lb (166kg)
Top speed	93mph (150km/h)

Gilera Saturno Sport

**Top speed
85mph**
137km/h

*Right: This 1950 model
Saturno Sport handled well,
thanks partly to its light
weight and rigid frame, but
shortly afterwards Gilera
uprated the model's chassis
with telescopic forks and
twin rear shocks.*

*Below: Simple styling and
Italian racing red
paintwork make the Sport a
very attractive roadster.
Removing lights and other
unnecessary accessories
converted it into a useful
racebike with minimal effort
and expense.*

 Lean, simple and finished in Italian Racing Red, the Saturno Sport was the high-performance model of the Milan-based firm's range of 500cc single-cylinder roadsters, which also included the softer Turismo model plus a police bike and a military machine.

Gilera's four-cylinder factory racers earned the company most of its fame by winning six world titles during the 1950s. But the Saturno was also an impressive performer on both road and track. Many owners simply removed the Sport's roadgoing parts such as lights and battery, then competed on Italian street circuits with considerable success.

For all its racy reputation, the Saturno was a simple machine. It was designed by Giuseppe Salmaggi, and was a development of the so-called 'eight-bolt' (*Otto Bulloni*) single that had been Gilera's main 500cc machine in the late 1930s. The first few Saturnos, introduced in 1940, were racing bikes. Gilera tester Massimo Masserini gave the model a good start when he won the prestigious Targa Florio road race, a test of endurance as well as speed, before production was interrupted by the outbreak of the Second World War.

Gilera began full-scale Saturno production in 1946. Its engine remained an air-cooled, vertical single, with long-stroke dimensions of 84 x 90mm – unchanged even on the racing versions – giving capacity of 499cc. It had pushrod-operated valves closed by hairpin springs, and a four-speed gearbox. The Sport had an aluminium cylinder head, 6:1 compression ratio, and produced 22bhp at 5000rpm. That gave it an advantage over the Touring model, with its iron head, lower compression and softer camshaft.

Gilera's Fabulous Fours

Gilera was founded in 1909 when Giuseppe Gellera, a young mechanic and hillclimber, produced a 317cc single-cylinder bike in his workshop near Milan. Gellera changed his name to Gilera, which he thought a better identity for his motorbike firm, and it quickly grew into one of Italy's most successful. Many Gileras were raced with good results in that period but the real glory came after Giuseppe Gilera bought the CNA Rondine (Swallow) bikes – supercharged 250cc fours that had won many races under previous ownership.

The marque's most glorious era was the 1950s, when its four-cylinder machines, designed by Piero Remor, dominated the 500cc world championship. Umberto Masetti won the title in 1950 and 1952, before Geoff Duke took over with a hat-trick for the Arcore factory. Libero Liberati added a sixth championship in 1957 before Gilera withdrew from racing, leaving the field open for MV Agusta to begin an even longer period of domination.

Top left: Gilera's powerful dohc four-cylinder grand prix bikes won six 500cc world titles, and led to many more because designer Piero Remor left to work for MV Agusta.

Far left: Saturno's crankcase is stamped with the name Arcore, the town near Milan where Gilera's factory was located before being closed in 1993.

Patented suspension system

Chassis layout of a 1950 Sport was mostly conventional, with a simple steel frame and girder forks, but rear suspension was by Gilera's unique patented system. An oval-section swingarm transmitted rear wheel movement, via two upright steel arms, to horizontal springs mounted in boxes above the swingarm. Each box contained a main spring to deal with bumps, plus a smaller rebound spring. Damping was provided by scissors-type friction units.

The Sport's performance did not approach that of Gilera's fiery, 110mph (177km/h) Sanremo competition single but, with plenty of low-rev torque and a top speed of about 85mph (137km/h), it was very lively. It also handled well in its original form, although by 1952 Gilera had updated the chassis with telescopic forks and twin rear shock absorbers.

Demand for the Saturno faded in the mid-

1950s, and production fell until it ended in 1959, when a total of almost 6500 had been built. By this time Gilera's management was more interested in the annual production of over 20,000 lightweight bikes with engines from 98 to 175cc. And crucially, the Sport's price of half a million lire would also buy a Fiat 500 car. That was one battle that even the Saturno Sport, with all its speed and spirit, could never win.

Above right: Gilera's patented rear suspension system used vertical steel arms to transfer wheel movement to springs that were mounted inside boxes above the swingarm. Damping was by scissors-type friction units to the rear.

Specification	Gilera Saturno Sport (1950)
Engine	Air-cooled ohv two-valve pushrod single
Capacity	499cc (84 x 90mm)
Maximum power	22bhp @ 5000rpm
Transmission	Four-speed, chain final drive
Frame	Steel single downtube
Suspension	Girder front; horizontal springs rear
Brakes	Drum front and rear
Weight	385lb (175kg)
Top speed	85mph (137km/h)

Ariel Square Four

**Top speed
100mph**
161km/h

*Below: The Square Four
4G MkI was a 997cc
machine that provided
plenty of smoothness and
comfort, if not outstanding
performance. This bike
dates from 1952, the year
before this model 'Squariel'
was replaced by the MkII
version, which featured
more power and improved
cooling, and was
distinguishable by its two
pairs of exhaust downpipes.*

'Ten to a hundred in top gear' was the
proud boast that Ariel used in its
advertising for the Square Four during the
1950s, emphasizing the machine's low-rev
refinement as well as its top speed of over 100mph
(161km/h). In fact, even the final version of the
Square Four was not as fast as its impressive
specification and high price suggested. It was more
of a luxurious – if rather unreliable – grand tourer
than a sports machine. But for many years Ariel's
flagship was one of the most glamorous bikes on
the road.

The Square Four went through numerous
redesigns during its long life, which lasted from
1931 to 1958. During that 27-year period, the
Ariel's engine capacity doubled, and its chassis and
styling were transformed. Yet the air-cooled square
four engine layout's advantages of power,
smoothness and compact size remained throughout
– as did its drawbacks of high production cost and
the difficulty of providing sufficient cooling for the
sheltered rear cylinders.

Cigarette packet sketch

Legend has it that this most exotic of motorcycles
was born after a gifted young engineer, Edward
Turner, had drawn up a novel square four engine
layout on the back of a cigarette packet and tried
unsuccessfully to sell the idea to a succession of
bike manufacturers. Turner, later to find lasting
fame at Triumph, eventually convinced Ariel chief
Jack Sangster that the square four concept was
sound, and was hired to put it into production.

Turner's design was basically a pair of parallel
twins, sharing the same cylinder head, block and
crankcase, with their crankshafts geared together.
This gave a naturally smooth-running engine, and
was so compact that the original 497cc unit could
be fitted into a frame very similar to that of Ariel's
current 500cc single. That first Square Four,
introduced in 1931, featured a chain-driven
overhead camshaft and exhaust manifolds integral
with the cylinder head, so that only two exhaust
pipes emerged from the engine. Turner's original
design had used an integral three-speed gearbox,

but the production bike had chain primary drive to a separate four-speed Burman box.

After one year of production the engine was enlarged to 597cc, giving extra power that was particularly welcomed by sidecar owners. In this form the Square Four produced 24bhp at 6000rpm, and stayed smooth to its top speed of 85mph (137km/h). But the 'Squariel' suffered from cooling and other problems. In 1937, after Turner had left for Triumph, Ariel introduced revised 597cc and 997cc models, known as the 4F and 4G, designed by new chief engineer Val Page.

The new engines featured more cylinder head finning plus a tunnel between the cylinders to allow cooling air to the rear of the block. Other changes included pushrod valve operation and longer-stroke dimensions. The larger 4G produced 34bhp with plenty of low-down torque. But as well as some unreliability it also suffered from mediocre handling, being too heavy for the plunger rear suspension system that had been adopted along with telescopic forks.

In 1953 Ariel introduced an uprated version, the 4G MkII, incorporating a new cylinder head complete with four instead of two downpipes. Cooling was improved by the air that now ran over the exhaust ports. Reshaped pistons helped raise power to 40bhp at 5000rpm, increasing top speed to over 105mph (169km/h). But Ariel never got round to introducing the liquid-cooled engine that

might have solved the longstanding overheating problem for good.

The reason for lack of further development was simple: Ariel, by now part of the BSA group, had made its controversial decision to abandon four-stroke production in favour of the two-stroke Leader commuter bike. In 1958, the year the Leader was launched, the four-cylinder bike was dropped from the range, and an era that had lasted for almost 30 years came to an end. No rider who had experienced the Square Four's unique blend of performance, smoothness and sophistication would forget it.

Above: Handling of the plunger-framed Square Four 4G Mk1 was not a strong point, partly due to the bike's substantial weight, but the Ariel provided a comfortable ride.

Below left: Twin downpipes gave the square-four engine a deceptively ordinary look. Despite heavy finning, cooling of the rear cylinders remained a problem throughout the model's life.

Left: The Square Four's good looks added to its glamour and appeal, and when the bike was running well there were few machines of the early 1950s that were more refined.

Specification	Ariel Square Four 4G MkI (1952)
Engine	Air-cooled ohv eight-valve pushrod square-four
Capacity	997cc (65 x 75mm)
Maximum power	34bhp @ 5400rpm
Transmission	Four-speed, chain final drive
Frame	Steel twin downtube
Suspension	Telescopic front; plunger rear
Brakes	Drum front and rear
Weight	433lb (196kg)
Top speed	100mph (161km/h)

BSA Gold Star Clubman

**Top speed
110mph**
177km/h

For a competition-hungry motorcyclist in the 1950s, a Gold Star DBD34 Clubman was arguably the ultimate machine, whether for racing on the Isle of Man, on short circuits or on the street in unofficial burn-ups between coffee bars. Lean, purposeful and unmistakably aggressive, the DBD34 Clubman was the last, fastest and best known version of a series of Gold Star singles that included 350 and 500cc bikes in touring, trials and scrambles form.

Unmistakable appearance

Its look was unmistakable: chrome-panelled fuel tank with BSA's famous star-in-a-red-circle badge, headlight jutting up above a narrow pair of clip-ons, swept-back exhaust pipe leading from a heavily finned vertical cylinder. And the performance was unique, too. First gear was good for no less than 60mph (97km/h). With the rider's chin brushing the big steering damper knob, the 'Goldie' had a genuine top speed of over 110mph (177km/h).

The Gold Star story began in 1937, when racer Wal Handley earned a Brooklands Gold Star award for lapping the banked Surrey track at over 100mph (161km/h) on BSA's 500cc M23 Empire Star. In the following year BSA produced a replica marketed under the name M24 Gold Star, the name signifying that each machine had been built using selected components, tuned and dyno-tested, with polished ports, conrod and crankcases.

That first Gold Star also had magnesium gearbox casings and aluminium cylinder head and barrel. Power output was 28bhp when fuelled by petrol, or 33bhp when tuned to run on alcohol. Buyers received a certified dyno chart from their machine, a custom that was maintained with Gold Stars throughout. But BSA management decided

Above: There were few more exciting bikes in the 1950s than a well-set-up Gold Star Clubman, which combined engine power with light, agile handling and powerful braking.

Right: This 1956-model DBD34 Clubman has all its go-faster components present and correct, including low clip-on bars, rearset footrests, filterless Amal carburettor and free-breathing megaphone exhaust. Not to mention the free-revving engine whose 42bhp peak output gave a top speed of well over 100mph (161km/h).

that to reduce costs the sports Gold Star should resemble the standard single as much as possible, so its chassis was relatively standard.

After the Second World War, BSA produced a competition bike called the B32, based on its pushrod single the B31. This was initially made for use in trials, but when fitted with an aluminium cylinder head and barrel its racing potential was clear. For 1949 BSA introduced the 350cc ZB32 Gold Star, followed a year later by the 500cc ZB34. Both were rapid, competitively priced and came with various options – four camshafts, three different sets of gears (standard, scrambles and racing), four compression ratios (for use with different fuels), and choice of fuel tanks, exhaust systems and wheels.

Suddenly the clubman racer had a machine well suited to road and track. At the TT in 1949, Harold Clark averaged over 75mph (121km/h) on a ZB32 to win the Junior Clubman's race, and in following years the Gold Star dominated both the 350cc Junior and 500cc Senior. In the 1955 Junior, no fewer than 33 of the 37 riders were on Goldies. But BSA's supremacy led to the Clubman's TT being dropped after the following year.

Competition wins

In 1956 BSA introduced the DBD34, which benefited from a development programme that had seen factory aces including Bill Nicholson ride Goldies to many wins in scrambles and trials. Competition-proven modifications, including steeper steering geometry, swingarm rear suspension and a new front brake, had subsequently been fitted to the production machine. The DBD34 also incorporated engine updates introduced by

Specification	BSA DBD34 Gold Star Clubman (1956)
Engine	Air-cooled ohv two-valve pushrod single
Capacity	499cc (85 x 88mm)
Maximum power	42bhp @ 7000rpm
Transmission	Four-speed, chain final drive
Frame	Steel twin downtube
Suspension	Telescopic front; twin shocks rear
Brakes	Drum front and rear
Weight	384lb (174kg)
Top speed	110mph (177km/h)

BSA's chief designer Bert Hopwood. It featured a big Amal GP carburettor, ultra-close-ratio gearbox and peak output of 42bhp at 7000rpm.

Other changes for the DBD34 Clubman's included the provision, for the first time, of the lights required by that season's racing regulations. That gave the Gold Star a deceptively normal appearance, but there was no doubting its suitability for serious competition. This was a true racebike on the road: demanding, temperamental and – most of all – very fast indeed.

Below left: The Gold Star tank badge dated back to the Brooklands Gold Star award won by BSA rider Wal Handley.

Below: Slim, purposeful lines not only helped the BSA's speed but made the bike look wonderfully purposeful too.

Vincent Black Shadow

**Top speed
125mph**
201km/h

*Below: The Black Shadow
Series C was the fastest
bike on the road in the late
1940s and early '50s, and
one of the most stylish.
Sadly for Philip Vincent and
his firm, the bike was so
expensive to produce that it
was not profitable despite
its high price.*

Vincent was motorcycling's greatest name in the years after the Second World War, and the Black Shadow was the firm's brightest star. With its powerful 998cc V-twin engine and fine-handling chassis, the Shadow was an exotic, superbly crafted and very rapid machine. Its top speed of over 120mph (193km/h) fully justified the advertising line, 'The World's Fastest Standard Motorcycle'.

The Black Shadow was a tuned version of Vincent's Rapide V-twin, itself a magnificent machine. Both models were high-performance roadburners, assembled in small numbers at Vincent's workshop at Stevenage in Hertfordshire by a small team led by Philip Vincent, the firm's founder, and Phil Irving, his Australian chief engineer.

Starting in business

Philip Vincent had begun by designing a novel form of sprung motorcycle frame in 1927, while an engineering student at Cambridge University. He left Cambridge and, with backing from his father, set up in business. To give his venture credibility, Vincent bought the name of HRD Motors. The initials were those of Howard Davies, a racer and engineer who had won the 1925 Senior TT on a bike he had built himself, but whose firm had not survived the recession. Vincent kept little of HRD apart from its paint scheme of black with gold trim, but he too intended to produce high-quality, technically innovative bikes.

Early Vincents were powered by proprietary engines from firms including JAP and Rudge. But in 1934 Vincent and Irving were furious when the unreliability of JAP's 'special' racing engines wrecked the firm's first attempt at the TT. Following their return from the Isle of Man, Irving designed a 499cc single-cylinder engine with an innovative 'high-camshaft' layout.

The basic Meteor single and sportier Comet, which was capable of 90mph (145km/h), were a success. They led to the first Rapide V-twin, introduced in 1936, which produced 45bhp from an engine whose cylinders were set at 47 degrees apart. Nicknamed the 'Snarling Beast', or 'plumber's nightmare' due to its external oil lines, it was fast but suffered from transmission problems caused by its torque.

Vincent replaced it after the war with the improved Series B Rapide. Its new unit-construction V-twin motor had cylinders at 50 degrees, and formed a stressed member of the chassis, so no downtubes were needed. It combined 110mph (177km/h) top speed with abundant mid-range torque, cruised effortlessly at high speed, and handled well. Twin drums on each wheel gave plenty of stopping power.

The tuned Black Shadow, launched in 1948, was faster still. To emphasize its extra performance the Shadow had a large Smiths speedometer calibrated to 150mph (241km/h), and black-finished cylinders and crankcases. A year later Vincent introduced the Series C range, in touring Rapide, sports Black Shadow and racing Black Lightning forms.

Vincents proved their performance worldwide. In 1949 American ace Rollie Free, riding a tuned Black Lightning, famously stripped to his swimming trunks to set a world record for unsupercharged bikes at 150.313mph (241.89km/h) on the Bonneville salt flats in Utah. Another hero was George Brown, who set speed records and won many sprints on Gunga Din, Nero and the supercharged Super Nero.

Vincent's problem was that the exotic, hand-built V-twins could not be produced at a profit. The firm struggled during the mid 1950s, and was forced to assemble Firefly engines and NSU lightweight bikes under licence. In 1955 Vincent launched the fully-enclosed Series D models, the Black Knight and tuned Black Prince. But the public was not yet ready for their black fibreglass bodywork, and sales slumped. Revised Rapide and Black Shadow models were reintroduced, but in vain. By the end of the year, Vincent's mighty beast had snarled its last.

Above: Black finish confirms that this is a Black Shadow engine, in a higher state of tune than the grey unit of the Rapide tourer.

Left: The side view shows off the front girder suspension plus one of the pair of rear shock units, located diagonally beneath the seat.

Below left: The fortunate Black Shadow rider was treated to the sight of a big Smith's speedometer that was calibrated to 150mph (241km/h).

Specification	Vincent Black Shadow Series C (1949)
Engine	Air-cooled ohv four-valve pushrod 50-degree V-twin
Capacity	998cc (84 x 90mm)
Maximum power	55bhp @ 5700rpm
Transmission	Four-speed, chain final drive
Frame	Steel spine
Suspension	Girder front; twin shocks rear
Brakes	Twin drums front and rear
Weight	458lb (208kg)
Top speed	125mph (201km/h)

Indian Chief

**Top speed
90mph**
145km/h

 An Indian Chief of the 1940s or early
'50s, with its big V-twin engine dwarfed
by enormous and often brightly painted
fenders over each wheel, is one of the most
instantly recognizable motorcycles ever produced.
Its story began long before those trademark fenders
were introduced, however. The Chief was the
heavyweight star of Indian's line-up for more than
30 years, following its introduction in 1922.

That first model, designed by Charles B.
Franklin, combined elements of the 988cc
Powerplus, which had been Indian's mainstay since
its introduction in 1916, and the smaller-engined
Scout, which had been launched in 1921. The
original Chief's blend of 988cc, 42-degree, side-
valve V-twin and Scout-style one-piece frame
resulted in good handling and a top speed of 85mph
(137km/h).

Even so, many riders believed the old adage
that there was no substitute for cubes, so just a year
later Indian enlarged the engine to 1213cc, or 74
cubic inches, to create the so-called 'Big Chief'.

Numerous updates were made in following years,
most notably the addition of a front brake in 1928.
Indian also equipped all its twins with a
re-circulating oil system, in place of the original
total loss arrangement, in 1933 – several years
before rival Harley followed suit.

High-performance version

In 1935 the Chief could be ordered with the
optional Y motor, whose aluminium heads and
larger fins gave better cooling, plus other options
including a four-speed gearbox instead of the
standard three-speeder. Later in the decade Indian
also offered a high-performance Bonneville motor
whose hot cams, polished ports and precision
ignition timing lifted top speed to an impressive
105mph (169km/h).

The mid-'30s Chief was also a good-looking
bike, and could be ordered in a wide variety of
colours because in 1930 Indian had been bought by
Du Pont, the manufacturing giant that had
connections in the paint industry. Around this time

Return of the Chief

Interest in Indian reawakened in the early 1990s when, with Harley sales booming, it became clear that there was room in the market for its old rival. The Indian name became a prized asset, fought over in law courts by a succession of firms, each of which claimed to have a new-generation Chief under development. When the dust settled in 1998, the winner emerged as the Indian Motorcycle Company, based at Gilroy in California. The following year, the firm began production of the Limited Edition 1999 Indian Chief, complete with trademark skirted fenders. Although the 'Harley clone' nature of its 1442cc V-twin engine displeased many traditionalists, the new Chief was well built and gave hope of a successful future for Indian.

Indian listed no fewer than 24 standard one- and two-colour schemes, plus the extra-cost option of any other colour from the Du Pont paint range.

But all was not well at the 'Wigwam', Indian's large Springfield factory, which by this time was running at only a fraction of its capacity. Indian struggled financially throughout the Depression-hit 1930s, and came close to bankruptcy in 1933. Although the company survived, it failed to compete with Harley by developing an overhead-valve V-twin to power the Chief, whose side-valve layout was becoming outdated.

The classical skirted-fender look was introduced in 1940. At the same time, Indian fitted the Chief with new cylinder heads and barrels whose larger cooling fins reduced running temperature. There was also a new frame, with plunger rear suspension. This resulted in an eye-catching, sweet-running and comfortable bike, but not a particularly quick one. The 558lb (253kg) Chief was fully 100lb (45kg) heavier than its 1935-model namesake. The days when an Indian rider

could 'dust' a Harley-mounted rival on the open road were over.

And although in 1950 Indian enlarged the V-twin engine to 1311cc (80ci), updated the chassis with telescopic forks in place of the previous girders, and fitted a conventional right-hand throttle as standard for the first time, it wasn't enough. Indian's financial problems, hastened by disastrous attempts to enter the small-capacity market, meant that relatively few Chiefs were built, and production ended in 1953.

Above left: The author takes a spin on a Chief owned by Californian-based Indian restorer and parts specialist Bob Stark.

Below left: Indian retained its traditional 42-degree cylinder angle from the days of its earliest V-twin engines.

Specification	Indian Chief (1953)
Engine	Air-cooled four-valve side-valve 42-degree V-twin
Capacity	1311cc (82.5 x 122mm)
Maximum power	50bhp @ 4800rpm
Transmission	Three-speed, chain final drive
Frame	Steel twin downtube
Suspension	Telescopic front; plunger rear
Brakes	Drum front and rear
Weight	570lb (259kg)
Top speed	90mph (145km/h)

Harley-Davidson Sportster

**Top speed
100mph**
161km/h

*Right: The Sportster's
883cc overhead-valve
V-twin engine produced
about 40bhp, giving 100mph
(161km/h) performance.
The so-called trumpet
jubilee horn was borrowed
from the big twin models.*

*Below: Early Sportsters are
hugely attractive bikes, with
a lean and simple profile
that is enhanced by two-
tone paint schemes and
chromed rear shocks.
Skyline blue and white was
an alternative to this bike's
Pepper red and black.*

It's a long time now since the Harley
Sportster lived up to its name. But there
was a time, in the few years after the
Sportster's release in 1957, when Milwaukee's lean
and handsome charger could show a clean rear
fender to just about any production bike on the
road. On straight-line acceleration away from a
stop-light, at any rate.

The feature that defined the XL was the
overhead-valve engine layout that replaced the
side-valve K series design. The new XL motor
retained the KH's 883cc capacity although it had a
wider bore and shorter stroke, which allowed
bigger valves and higher revs. Other features of
that first Sportster model were its cast iron cylinder
heads, and the 'Sportster' logo cast into the
engine's primary drive cover. The bike had two-
tone paint, telescopic forks, twin shocks with
chrome covers, and a single sprung saddle.

Cycle magazine found the XL capable of just
over 100mph (161km/h), and reported that the XL
had 'terrific acceleration all through the rev range',
and that 'high cruising speeds can be sustained
indefinitely without effort from the ruggedly

constructed engine.' Although such performance
was not a huge improvement on that of the side-
valve KHK model, the XL was an instant hit,
selling almost twice the number that the K-series
models had managed in 1956.

Growing reputation

A legend had been born, and in subsequent years it
quickly grew, through a number of Sportster
variants, many of which adopted the tiny factory-

option peanut gas tank that had originally been fitted to Harley's little two-stroke 125cc Model S or Hummer. There was the off-road XLC, stripped of lights and with open pipes; and the XLH with its tuned engine. Fastest of all was the XLCH – originally a California-only dirt-bike with no lights *and* hot motor, but in 1959 broadened to a full '50-state' road-legal model whose lean, basic, engine-dominated look and thunderous performance epitomized the Sportster's appeal.

From 1960 the hotter H engine was used for all Sportsters, and subsequent years saw other modifications including the adoption of bigger drum brakes, a headlamp nacelle, 12 volt electrics, a Tillotson instead of Linkert carburettor, and the aforementioned hot cams. Sportster buyers in 1968 could choose either the raw-and-simple XLCH or the XLH, which came with an electric starter for the first time.

The modified engine cases required for the electric foot resulted in the wheelbase lengthening, and new parts, including a bigger battery, increased the bike's dry weight to a substantial 519lb (235kg). But the XLH was still a very rapid motorbike. That V-twin punch and the deep soundtrack were totally addictive, and the Harley's ability to cruise at an indicated 70mph (113km/h), feeling relaxed and reasonably smooth, was undeniably impressive.

Harley continued to change the Sportster over the years, generally improving it slightly,

Specification	Harley-Davidson XL Sportster (1957)
Engine	Air-cooled ohv four-valve pushrod 45-degree V-twin
Capacity	883cc (76.2 x 96.8mm)
Maximum power	40bhp @ 5500rpm
Transmission	Four-speed, chain final drive
Frame	Steel twin downtube
Suspension	Telescopic front; twin shocks rear
Brakes	Drum front and rear
Weight	463lb (210kg)
Top speed	100mph (161km/h)

occasionally taking a step backwards (as with the ugly boat-tail seat, introduced in 1971 and quickly dropped). In 1974 the engine was bored out to 1000cc and a disc front brake was introduced. The 1978-model Anniversary Sportster featured cast wheels, twin discs and black paint. Other variants included the XLS Roadster of 1980, with its big tank and high bars; the rapid but unreliable XR-1000 special of 1983; and, most significantly, the 1986-model XLH 883, with its Evolution engine in the traditional 54 cubic inch (883cc) capacity.

The Sportster has remained successful into the 21st century, with innovations such as the 1200cc motor and the low-slung Hugger. Recent models have combined that unmistakable XLH look with belt final drive and Milwaukee's improved quality control. But for all the modern models' style and efficiency, there's one area where they are no match for the old Sportsters: they can't outrun the fastest opposition of the day.

Below left: This XL engine was uprated to XLH specification in 1958, when larger valves, lighter tappets and higher 9:1 compression ratio added 5bhp, giving a total of 45bhp. Later models gained style with a tiny peanut tank but lost this bike's Sportster chaincase logo.

Below: In recent years the Sportster has been hugely popular while not living up to its name, but the 1996 model XL1200S Sportster Sport gave a performance boost with its uprated suspension and brakes.

Triumph T120 Bonneville

**Top speed
110mph**
177km/h

*Right: Handling was less
of a Bonneville strong point
than engine performance,
but a 1961-model T120R
was well suited to rapid
cornering.*

*Below: Few Triumph
enthusiasts agree on which
Bonneville model is best or
most attractive, but this
1961 model would get
plenty of votes.*

 The Bonneville remains Triumph's most famous model of all, and for very good reason. Launched in 1959 as a hotted-up, twin-carb version of the Meriden firm's existing 650cc vertical twin, the T120 Bonneville was advertised as offering 'the highest performance available today from a standard production motorcycle' – and the Bonnie lived up to its billing.

For much of the following decade the T120 was as fast as any production bike on the road, and it was a long-lasting hit for Triumph. Bonneville-based bikes were also raced successfully all around the world, from the Isle of Man TT to American dirt tracks. The Bonnie was repeatedly updated, enlarged to 750cc, and survived into the 1980s. No wonder John Bloor's reborn Triumph concern chose the famous name for its new generation parallel twin, launched in 2001.

Back in 1959, the name Bonneville was evocative of speed and excitement for a different

reason. Triumph's legendary boss Edward Turner chose it in honour of the record-breaking run by Johnny Allen, who in 1956 had taken a streamlined, Triumph twin-engined machine to 214mph (344km/h) at the Bonneville salt flats in Utah, USA. The American market was Triumph's biggest, and the name fitted the new bike perfectly.

The original T120 was relatively simple for Triumph to develop. Its format of 649cc parallel twin, with pushrod valve operation, four-speed gearbox and 360-degree crankshaft was that of the Tiger 110. In 1958 the Tiger had been available with an optional cylinder head with splayed inlet ports, for fitment of twin carburettors, plus a list of optional tuning parts including high-performance camshafts and Amal racing carbs.

Following demand from its US distributors for a high-performance model, Triumph incorporated hot cams and twin, filterless Amal Monobloc carbs in the new T120, increasing peak output by 4bhp to 46bhp. Initially the Bonneville, which was conceived in such a hurry that it wasn't even included in the firm's 1959 catalogue, retained the Tiger's headlamp nacelle and touring handlebars. For 1960 it gained a separate headlamp shell and sportier mudguards, plus a redesigned twin-cradle frame that gave steeper steering geometry and a shorter wheelbase.

The frame was strengthened for 1961, by which time the Bonneville had become firmly established as a stylish and fast road-burner. British magazine *Motor Cycling* wrote in June 1961 of the 'outstanding acceleration and high top speed – without temperament' of a bike that lapped a banked test-track at an impressive average of 108mph (174km/h). Three months later the magazine tripped the timing lights at 117mph (188km/h) on the same bike, now revving higher after being fitted with Triumph's high-performance option of 'chopped' Amal Monobloc carburettors sharing a single float bowl.

Easy handling and good looks

The Bonneville was regularly updated over the next decade, notably with the adoption of a unit-construction engine and gearbox in 1963. Chassis stability did not always match engine performance, but the Bonnie remained much loved for its light weight, easy handling and good looks. In 1971 the twin gained a new 'oil-in-frame' chassis, which was much criticized until lowered a year later. In 1973 Triumph increased capacity to 744cc to produce the T140 Bonneville, which was more flexible, if no faster and less smooth.

Bonnevilles were raced with great success, notably in the Isle of Man, where John Hartle won the production TT in 1967, and Malcolm Uphill set the first production 100mph (161km/h) lap on the way to victory in 1969. During the 1960s the T120 took four wins in the annual 500-mile (805km) production race at Thruxton and Brands Hatch, with riders including Triumph tester Percy Tait. The Bonnie was still competitive on the track in 1978, when Steve Trasler's T140 beat the Japanese fours to win the British production championship.

Above left: The Silver Jubilee Bonneville of 1977 was a special edition of the 750cc T140, built by Triumph to celebrate Queen Elizabeth II's 25 years on the British throne. The Bonnie was old-fashioned compared to Japanese rivals, though not without performance and charm.

Above right: The Bonneville made a return in 2001, when John Bloor's reborn Triumph firm introduced a roadster twin, styled after a 1968-model T120 but with a modern 790cc, dohc eight-valve engine. Ironically the new 61bhp Bonnie was no faster than many old models.

Specification	Triumph T120 Bonneville (1961)
Engine	Air-cooled four-valve ohv pushrod parallel twin
Capacity	649cc (71 x 82mm)
Maximum power	46bhp @ 6500rpm
Transmission	Four-speed, chain final drive
Frame	Steel twin downtube
Suspension	Telescopic front; twin shocks rear
Brakes	Drum front and rear
Weight	403lb (183kg) wet
Top speed	110mph (177km/h)

Velocette Venom Thruxton

**Top speed
105mph**
169km/h

*Right: Thruxton's 499cc
motor used a big Amal
carburettor and new
cylinder head to increase
power output to 40bhp.*

*Below: Features including
low handlebars, sticking-up
twin instruments, big front
drum brake and humped
seat gave the Thruxton a
suitably racy appearance.*

 The Velocette marque's speciality was
single-cylinder roadsters that were closely
related to racing machines, and the fastest
and most famous of them all was the Venom
Thruxton. Sleek, singleminded and ready to take to
the track with minimal modification, the 500cc
Thruxton was in many respects the ultimate street
racer of the 1960s.

Essentially a tuned and race-kitted version of
the Venom, Velocette's standard (though still
distinctly sporty and uncompromising) large-
capacity model, the Thruxton was named after the
Hampshire circuit where the marque had been
consistently successful in long-distance production
racing. Indeed, the model owed its existence
directly to the competition experience that the firm
from Hall Green in Birmingham had gained, most
notably at the gruelling and prestigious Thruxton
500-mile (805km) event.

Racy Clubman trim

Since 1956 the firm's main sports model had been
the Venom, powered by a 499cc pushrod single
engine with square dimensions of 86 x 86mm. Since
1960 it had been available in racier Clubman trim,
with low bars, high compression piston and other
mods. Then, in 1964, the factory offered a high-
performance kit. This comprised a new cylinder
head, with narrower valve angle, larger inlet valve
and revised porting; plus a big Amal Grand Prix
carburettor, which necessitated fuel and oil tanks
cut away to accommodate its gaping bell-mouth.

For the following year, Velocette incorporated
the kit into the new Venom Thruxton model, which
also featured a suitably shaped tank – finished in
striking silver – plus clip-on handlebars, humped
racing seat, rearset footrests, alloy wheel rims, and
a twin-leading-shoe front drum brake with a big
scoop for cooling air. At a few pence under £370
the Thruxton was expensive (Velo's hand-built
bikes were never cheap, anyway), but it promised a
seriously competitive level of performance.

The Venom Thruxton did not disappoint. Its
uprated engine produced a claimed 40bhp at
6200rpm, which was only a few horsepower up on
the Clubman but was enough to push the single's
top speed to 105mph (169km/h). Despite its high
state of tune the big thumper was tractable, too,

Left: The Thruxton's large-capacity fuel tank was initially finished in silver, and incorporated a cut-out in its base to allow room for the carburettor. The fishtail silencer is a Velocette trademark that dates back many decades.

Below: The idiosyncratic Thruxton is not one of the easiest of bikes to live with, but when running well it delivers a thrilling blend of long-legged cruising ability and stable high-speed handling.

pulling from 2000rpm in top gear and happily ambling along at 3000rpm with plenty of instant acceleration in hand. Inevitably there was some vibration, but this cleared at about 4500rpm, allowing reasonably comfortable 90mph (145km/h) cruising on the open road.

For such a race-bred machine the handling was not flawless, as the rear suspension generated some instability at racing speeds. At 390lb (177kg) the Thruxton was not especially light, either. Typically for such a sporty single, it was also hard to start and was prone to loose bolts due to vibration.

But this was exactly the sort of high-performance, race-derived and uncompromising machine that Velocette enthusiasts preferred. The Thruxton was a success, and more than 1100 were built over the next few years; some of them, by popular request, in Velocette's traditional black-and-gold colouring. The model finished first and second in its class at the Production TT, too, both bikes lapping at almost 90mph (145km/h).

Sadly, the Thruxton was untypical of Velocette production, because for years the firm had been moving away from its traditional customer base, with disastrous result. During the 1950s, production of the four-stroke singles had almost been abandoned in favour of the lightweight, two-stroke, fully-enclosed LE, which had failed to sell. The Viceroy, a 250cc scooter, was even more of a flop. Even the plucky Venom Thruxton could not save Velocette, and in 1971 production ended for good.

Specification	Velocette Venom Thruxton (1965)
Engine	Air-cooled ohv two-valve pushrod single
Capacity	499cc (86 x 86mm)
Maximum power	40bhp @ 6200rpm
Transmission	Four-speed, chain final drive
Frame	Steel single downtube
Suspension	Telescopic front; twin shocks rear
Brakes	Drum front and rear
Weight	390lb (177kg)
Top speed	105mph (169km/h)

Norton Commando

**Top speed
115mph**
185km/h

*Right: The stylish
Commando S, with its high-
level exhaust pipes on the
left, was introduced in 1969
mainly to gain sales in
America, where off-road
riding was popular.*

*Below: The classic
Commando look combines
the angled-forward parallel
twin engine with Norton's
so-called Fastback
tailpiece, designed more for
style than pillion comfort.*

For many riders, the Norton Commando
was the ultimate bike of the late 1960s
and early '70s. It combined a powerful,
torquey engine with a fine-handling chassis that
minimized the traditional British parallel twin
problem of vibration.

The original Commando, launched in 1968, was
powered by a 745cc pushrod-operated parallel twin
motor that was based on that of the previous Atlas,
but was angled forward in the chassis instead of
positioned vertically. Changes included higher
compression ratio and a single-plate diaphragm
clutch. Peak power was 58bhp at 6800rpm.

But it was the chassis that made the Commando
special; more specifically, the 'Isolastic' system of
rubber mounting that promised to get rid of the
vibration that had plagued the Atlas and other
larger-capacity British parallel twins. The system,
developed by a team headed by former Rolls-Royce
engineer Dr Stefan Bauer, attached the engine to
the frame by rubber mounts. The frame itself
comprised a large main spine plus twin downtubes.

Rear engine plates were also rubber-mounted,
isolating the motor while allowing the frame's
spine to counter torsional stresses.

The Commando, which combined this chassis
innovation with striking styling including a
streamlined 'Fastback' tailpiece, made an
immediate impact. The bike was fast, with a top
speed of 115mph (185km/h) and strong mid-range

Specification	Norton Commando (1968)
Engine	Air-cooled ohv four-valve pushrod parallel-twin
Capacity	745cc (73 x 89mm)
Maximum power	58bhp @ 6800rpm
Transmission	Four-speed, chain final drive
Frame	Steel spine with twin downtubes
Suspension	Telescopic front; twin shock rear
Brakes	Drum front and rear
Weight	420lb (191kg)
Top speed	115mph (185km/h)

acceleration. More to the point, the Isolastic frame really worked. Firstly, it succeeded in isolating the rider from vibration effectively, at least so long as the Isolastic bushes were well maintained. And in combination with Norton's Roadholder forks and Girling shocks, it gave handling that was well up to the old firm's traditional high standards.

Terrific power

Magazine tests were full of praise. *Motor Cycle*, reviewing the Commando's impact several months after its launch, summed-up: 'The terrific power of the modified 745cc Atlas twin was a new experience now it was rubber-mounted in an ingenious frame which did, in fact, virtually eliminate the effects of high-frequency vibration. The sceptics retired to swallow their doubts. Overnight the Commando became the most sought-after large-capacity roadster on the market.'

After a further 2000-mile (3200km) trip, the tester concluded that the Norton 'gave a new dimension to the sort of riding we have known on parallel twins in the past 20 years'. The Commando proceeded to win the *Motor Cycle News* Machine of the Year competition five years in a row. American riders also took to the Commando which, for that very important market, was fitted with high, wide handlebars.

Americans benefited from some of the special versions that Norton developed over the next few years, notably the 1971 model Commando SS, a street scrambler with a small gas tank and high-level pipes. The Commando Hi-Rider model added a chopper-style seat to its similar tank and high-level bars. Norton went the opposite way with the Combat Commando, which had flatter bars to suit its tuned, high-compression 65bhp motor. But the

Combat was an embarrassment. Its main bearings could not handle the extra power, and Norton's hurried attempts to fix the problem with a new head gasket backfired when these started leaking.

The factory had much more success in 1973, when the engine was bored-out to create the Commando 850, available in standard Roadster and large-tanked Interstate options. The bigger motor's extra torque gave a welcome performance boost to a parallel twin that by now was competing against Japanese multis. But the British bike's limitations were highlighted by Norton's difficulty in providing a reliable electric starter. By now parent company Norton Villiers Triumph was in financial trouble, and production finally ceased in 1977.

Above left: The Commando gave Norton fresh life, but even by enlarging the original 745cc engine to 828cc it could not keep the pushrod twin competitive in the 1970s.

Below: This 1972 specification machine was assembled in 1995 from new parts by British Norton parts specialist Fair Spares, one of several firms to offer freshly built Commandos.

Triumph Trident

**Top speed
125mph**
201km/h

*Right: The 1975-model
T160 Trident, with its
angled-forward engine and
stylish two-tone paint
scheme, was generally
regarded as a much more
handsome machine than the
original T150.*

*Below: Angular lines,
unusual paint scheme and
distinctive 'raygun' silencers
gave the T150 Trident an
old-fashioned look that was
unpopular with many
Triumph enthusiasts.*

When Triumph launched the T150 Trident
in 1969, the 750cc triple's blend of
smooth power and stable handling made it
one of the fastest bikes on the road. In road-racing,
too, Trident-based machines scored many notable
victories, not least on the high-speed banking of
Daytona. But the triple was never the success that
Triumph had hoped, partly due to its angular
styling, aquamarine paintwork and unusual 'raygun' silencers, all of which were especially
unpopular in the States.

The Trident's design was also very much of the
1960s, in contrast to that of Honda's more refined
CB750 four, which was launched a few months
later. The 740cc triple had pushrod valve operation,
and produced 58bhp at 7250rpm. The chassis was
heavily based on that of Triumph's twins, including
the frame which was a strengthened version of their
single-downtube unit. Front forks, borrowed from
the twins, had stiffer springs to cope with the
triple's extra weight. The drum front brake also
came from a 650cc twin.

High-speed cruising

The Trident was certainly fast. Its 125mph
(201km/h) top speed and sub 14-second quarter-
mile time were mighty impressive in 1969. So too
was the smooth power delivery that allowed
sustained high-speed cruising, and which made the
Trident a much better long-distance bike than
contemporary twins. The Trident could crack
100mph (161km/h) in third gear, and show its

fancy silencers to just about any vehicle on the road. For a big bike its handling was good, too.

Triumph attempted to uprate the Trident over the years, although the firm's financial problems ensured that many mods were merely cosmetic. The disappointing front brake was changed to a conical drum in 1971, then to a single disc. Styling changes included a smaller fuel tank that combined with the Trident's thirst to give very poor range. (Many American dealers threw away the standard tank and exhausts, fitting parts from the twin to make the Trident more appealing.)

Trident performance suffered when the 1973 model's revised carburation and silencers, introduced due to tightening emission laws, resulted in 10mph (16km/h) being lost from the top speed. Equally seriously, the Trident never really recovered from its early reputation for unreliability – much of which was caused by poor assembly rather than flawed design. Those problems and its high price meant that the Trident never had much chance of success.

In 1975, Triumph replaced the T150 with the redesigned T160 Trident. This was a handsome machine whose engine incorporated many new features including an electric starter and left-foot

Specification	Triumph T150 Trident (1969)
Engine	Air-cooled ohv six-valve pushrod triple
Capacity	740cc (67 x 70mm)
Maximum power	58bhp @ 7250rpm
Transmission	Four-speed, chain final drive
Frame	Steel single downtube
Suspension	Telescopic front; twin shocks rear
Brakes	Drum front and rear
Weight	468lb (212kg)
Top speed	125mph (201km/h)

gearchange. The new bike's frame angled the motor forward in the style of BSA's Rocket Three. Its layout was influenced by Triumph's works production race triples including the legendary Slippery Sam, which won five consecutive Isle of Man TT Production races from 1971 to '75.

Finally, the Trident was the bike it might have been all along, with good looks, excellent performance, fine handling and a smooth ride. Although it had some reliability problems, and a high price, the T160 was the fastest, most sophisticated British bike yet. But it did not last long. By the end of 1975, production had ended following the collapse of parent company Norton Villiers Triumph.

Below left: Triumph's three-cylinder engine was powerful and reasonably smooth, but was very much a design from the 1960s. The pushrod triple's lack of sophistication was further emphasized when compared with Honda's CB750 unit, with its overhead camshaft, additional cylinder, electric starter and superior reliability.

American Beauty: The Stunning X-75

The most stylish of Triumph's triples was the 1973 model X-75 Hurricane, created by young freelance American designer Craig Vetter. Commissioned by Triumph's American distributor, initially without the factory's knowledge, it was everything that the T150 wasn't: slim, curvy, and eye-catching. Geared for acceleration and with a tiny fuel tank, it was impractical – but unbeatable away from the lights. Fewer than 1200 were built, but decades later the Hurricane is remembered as an icon of two-wheeled style.

Honda CB750

**Top speed
123mph**
198km/h

With a top speed of over 120mph (193km/h) and a standing quarter-mile time of under 13 seconds, Honda's original CB750 four was one of the fastest and hardest-accelerating bikes on the roads in the early 1970s. But it was not sheer speed alone that made the Honda such a huge success back then; nor that caused it to be widely regarded as the most important machine that the motorcycle industry has yet produced.

More than simply sheer performance, it was the CB750's unmatched sophistication that made it special. When it arrived in 1969, the Honda was the first mass-produced four, and it incorporated refinements including an electric starter, disc front brake and five-speed gearbox. As well as being competitively priced, it was also impressively well built. By this time, a generation of motorcyclists had grown up on smaller Hondas, and were confident that the Japanese firm's bikes would be mechanically reliable, and would have good electrics and no oil leaks. They would not be disappointed by the glamorous four.

Influenced by racebikes

Of all the Honda's attributes, that powerful, smooth-running engine was the most important. The 736cc unit's design was influenced by Honda's multi-cylinder racebikes of the 1960s, although the roadster relied on a single overhead camshaft and two valves per cylinder, in contrast to the racers with their twin cams and four valves per pot. The Honda's capacity of 736cc came from its relatively long-stroke dimensions of 61 x 63mm, which helped reduce width.

Above: The original CB750 had conventional styling and fairly high handlebars, but its disc front brake and especially its four-cylinder engine brought a new level of sophistication and performance to motorcycling. More than three decades later, its influence is still clear in the design of modern superbikes.

Right: Most of the first fours to be produced were sold in America, where the model went on sale in mid-1969. This bike, built in October of that year, was the first to be sold in Britain and was registered in January 1970.

Tuned For Speed – The CB750F2

Honda was slow to update the CB750 in the 1970s, despite the arrival of rivals including Kawasaki's more powerful 900cc Z1. In fact the CB was detuned over the years to reduce emissions. Even the 1976 model CB750F1, which looked sporty with flat handlebars and bright yellow paint, could manage only 115mph (185km/h). But a year later came the CB750F2. Its black-painted engine had bigger valves, high-lift camshaft, redesigned combustion chamber and produced 73bhp, an extra 6bhp. Chassis improvements included a strengthened frame, new suspension and triple disc brakes. With top speed of over 120mph (193km/h) and excellent handling, the F2 was the last and best of Honda's single-cam 750s.

The motor was angled slightly forward in a steel, twin cradle frame, which held gaitered front forks and twin rear shock absorbers. Honda created the initial CB750 as an all-rounder, aiming it primarily at the US market. It was a physically large machine with a wide seat. It also had fairly high handlebars, but the wind-blown riding position did not prevent it from being well suited to cruising at speed.

Chassis performance did not quite match that of the engine, with the flex-prone steel frame causing a few wobbles under very hard riding. But by early 1970s standards the Honda's handling was good. Although quite heavy, the four carried its weight well, thanks partly to firm suspension. Its disc front brake gave an edge in both image and performance over rival firms' drums, too.

Demand for the CB750 was huge, notably in America, where most of the early production was sold. Honda even got a barely necessary marketing boost from competition success, when veteran ace Dick Mann won the 1970 Daytona 200 on a modified CB750. *Cycle World* introduced the Honda as 'the ultimate weapon in one-upmanship – a magnificent, muscle-bound racer for the road', and concluded in its road test that the CB750 was 'the very best road bike in the world'.

Few who rode it at the time disagreed with that. And, as four-cylinder Japanese superbikes began to dominate the two-wheeled scene through the 1970s and '80s, the Honda's enormous influence became apparent. After the CB750, high-performance motorcycling would never be the same again.

Left: Honda's 736cc straight-four powerplant had a chain-driven single overhead camshaft and eight valves. Carburation and exhaust changes necessary to meet tightening emissions legislation meant that its 67bhp output was initially reduced, rather than increased, in subsequent years. Although the Honda had an electric starter, it was also fitted with a kick-starter as a back-up.

Specification	Honda CB750 (1969)
Engine	Air-cooled sohc eight-valve four
Capacity	736cc (61 x 63mm)
Maximum power	67bhp @ 8000rpm
Transmission	Five-speed, chain final drive
Frame	Steel twin downtube
Suspension	Telescopic front; twin shocks rear
Brakes	Single disc front; drum rear
Weight	506lb (230kg) wet
Top speed	123mph (198km/h)

MV Agusta 750 Sport

**Top speed
115mph**
185km/h

Right: MV's potent four-cylinder engine, with its gear-driven twin overhead cams, owed much to the firm's all-conquering grand prix racebikes.

Below: This Sport, built as Phil Read was winning MV's 16th consecutive 500cc world championship in 1973, has the disc front brake introduced that year.

 The 750 Sport with which MV Agusta announced its arrival as a manufacturer of roadgoing superbikes was a long time coming, but it proved well worth the wait. The Sport, with its handsome lines, potent 743cc, dohc engine and impressive chassis specification, was stunning: a high performance roadster that was based on the Italian marque's all-conquering 500cc factory racebikes.

When the Sport reached production in the early 1970s, the small firm from Gallarate, near Milan, was nearing the end of a remarkable era of racetrack domination. MV's unbroken string of 500cc world titles stretched back to 1958, with riders including John Surtees, Mike Hailwood and Giacomo Agostini. For all this time the firm's autocratic boss, Count Domenico Agusta, had refused to produce a roadgoing version of the four-cylinder 'Gallarate fire engines'.

Instead, MV production had concentrated on the small-capacity singles with which Domenico had entered the motorcycle business in 1945, when the Agusta aircraft company was looking for a new direction at the end of the Second World War. Although a stylish 500cc four called the R19 Turismo had generated plenty of interest when

displayed at the Milan Show as early as 1950, it had not been produced. When MV did build a roadgoing four, it was an ugly 600cc, shaft-drive tourer that barely managed 100mph (161km/h) and sold in tiny numbers.

Designed for speed

The 750 Sport was dramatically different. This was an uncompromising sports machine. It had low handlebars, rearset footrests, bold red, white and blue paintwork, a humped race-style seat, a quartet of unfiltered Dell'Orto carburettors, and four shiny megaphone pipes. Its engine was based on that of the tourer, but bored out to 743cc, and tuned with higher compression plus larger exhaust valves.

It also produced considerably more power, its peak of 65bhp at 7900rpm being 13bhp up on that of the 600. Like that bike and MV's racers, the Sport used gear drive to its twin overhead cams. Its crankcases were sandcast, in aluminium rather than the racers' magnesium. The competition motor had no generator, so a combined starter/dynamo was added beneath the engine and connected by two belts.

Frame design owed more to the 600 than to the racebikes, as the Sport had one instead of two top tubes. The Sport also surprised many people by retaining the 600's shaft final drive system, reportedly because Count Domenico did not want the bike to be raced for fear that privateers would damage his factory team's reputation. But the Sport was equipped with top-quality cycle parts, including Ceriani forks and twin shocks, and Borrani alloy wheel rims. Early models had a big four-leading-shoe Grimeca front drum brake; later versions had twin discs.

For the few riders who could afford one, the Sport was a magnificent bike. Top speed was about 115mph (185km/h), rather than the factory's optimistic claim of 140mph (225km/h), but that was fast enough. And the MV's smooth acceleration, plus especially the aural treat of rustling motor and howling exhaust note, made every trip an event. Handling and braking were good, too, even if the heavy, shaft-drive Sport had nowhere near the agility or stability of MV's racers. Some owners later fitted chain-drive conversions from former MV race team boss Arturo Magni, who set up in business near Gallarate.

MV's dominance of the grand prix circuits was eventually halted by the Japanese two-strokes in 1975. The firm quit racing, and its roadsters did not last much longer. Despite their high prices, neither the Sport nor the later America and Monza fours were financially viable. Their intricate, hand-built engines were very costly to assemble, and production numbers were very low. By the end of the 1970s, MV had abandoned motorcycles to concentrate on helicopter production.

Left: The Sport's race-style full fairing was available as a factory option, as were a half fairing and a perspex flyscreen. The roadster's red, white and blue paint scheme did not match that of the scarlet 'Gallarate fire engine' grand prix bikes, but contributed to the MV's racy look.

Below: Despite its heavy drive-shaft assembly and a frame that was less rigid than that of the racers, the Sport handled reasonably well, especially when fitted with later Marzocchi shocks with remote damping fluid reservoirs, as is the case with this otherwise standard machine.

Specification	MV Agusta 750 Sport (1973)
Engine	Air-cooled dohc eight-valve four
Capacity	743cc (65 x 56mm)
Maximum power	65bhp at 7900rpm
Transmission	Five-speed, shaft final drive
Frame	Steel twin downtube
Suspension	Telescopic front; twin shocks rear
Brakes	Twin discs front; drum rear
Weight	506lb (230kg) dry
Top speed	115mph (185km/h)

Kawasaki Z1

**Top speed
132mph**
212km/h

Below: As well as being by far the world's most powerful production motorcycle, the Z1 was a handsome machine that screamed power and speed despite its high handlebars and a thick dual seat. This 1974-model Z1-A differs from the previous year's original Z1 in its paint scheme and alloy, instead of black, engine finish.

They called it the King, and in the mid-1970s there was no disputing that Kawasaki's Z1 ruled the roads. When the 903cc four was launched in 1973, its top speed of over 130mph (210km/h) put the new bike 10mph (16km/h) ahead of Honda's CB750, its closest challenger. The Kawasaki was also more than a second quicker through the standing quarter mile, and just happened to be good-looking and very reliable too. No wonder it was an instant smash hit.

The Z1's early story is one of triumph over near disaster. Kawasaki originally intended to build a 750cc four, and was close to completing work on the project, codenamed New York Steak, when Honda unveiled the CB750. Once the initial disappointment had faded, Kawasaki's engineers realized that they now had the advantage of knowing what they had to beat. They enlarged their own engine to 903cc, and returned four years later to do just that.

Horsepower advantage

There was never any doubt that the Z1 engine, which featured twin overhead cams, working eight valves via bucket-and-shim adjustment, would have a substantial advantage of the smaller, sohc CB750 unit, which had changed little in the meantime. With a maximum output of 82bhp at 8500rpm, the Kawasaki motor was 15bhp more powerful, and produced considerably more low-rev torque too. It sat near vertically in a twin-downtube frame whose forks held a 19-inch wheel and single disc brake.

If the Z1's chassis specification was nothing out of the ordinary, its styling gained some extra advantage. Although the Kawasaki was undeniably big and heavy, weighing 542lb (246kg) with fuel, it was very well proportioned. Its curved fuel tank, small sidepanels and rear duck-tail behind the dual seat gave a stylish, vibrant look that was totally in keeping with its performance.

Not that the riders of any other bike got to see

A Faster Four – The Z1-R

Kawasaki's answer to increased challenges from rival Japanese fours in 1978 was the Z1-R, an uprated version of the current Z1000. The most obvious change was the bikini fairing, whose angular lines were echoed in the fuel tank and bodywork. The standard 1015cc engine remained, but bigger carbs and a four-into-one pipe increased output by 6bhp to 90bhp. Chassis updates included a braced frame, retuned suspension, cast wheels and revamped brakes. Top speed was increased to 130mph (209km/h), and the fairing boosted high-speed comfort, though not stability. Handling at lower speeds was marginally better, too. Overall this was the best big Kawasaki yet.

more than the back of the fast-disappearing Z1 on the road. Its acceleration was brutal by contemporary standards, with the big twin-cam motor churning out smooth, strong torque throughout its rev range. There was plenty of scope to make it faster still, too, as many tuners and racers soon confirmed.

Handling was a different matter. In normal use the Z1 gave no problem, and was even fairly comfortable despite its high handlebars. Pushed harder, the awesome motor was sometimes too much for the chassis, causing high-speed instability. Many owners fitted steering dampers and aftermarket rear shocks, which helped. Better still was a frame kit from a specialist such as Harris, Martin, Egli or Bakker.

Most owners found the Z1 plenty good enough as it was. Such was its performance lead that Kawasaki's only changes for the first two years were cosmetics and minor details. In 1976 a second front disc brake, previously an optional extra, became standard fitment, while smaller carbs and more restrictive pipes (to reduce emissions for the US market) reduced peak power slightly. The bike also gained a new name, becoming the Z900. One other thing didn't change: its status as the two-wheeled King of the road.

Above left: Kawasaki's dohc four-cylinder engine not only outclassed all opposition with its 82bhp power output, it also proved remarkably reliable.

Left: The Z1's high handlebars made life uncomfortable for its rider at high speed, and did nothing to aid stability.

Specification	Kawasaki Z1 (1973)
Engine	Air-cooled dohc eight-valve four
Capacity	903cc (66 x 66mm)
Maximum power	82bhp @ 8500rpm
Transmission	Five-speed, chain final drive
Frame	Steel twin downtube
Suspension	Telescopic front; twin shocks rear
Brakes	Single disc front; drum rear
Weight	542lb (246kg) wet
Top speed	132mph (212km/h)

BMW R90S

**Top speed
125mph**
201km/h

*Right: Dell'Orto pumper
carbs and high-compression
motor raised the 898cc
boxer motor's output to
67bhp.*

*Below: The R90S's fairing
was as important as its
engine in increasing
practical performance.*

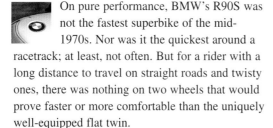

On pure performance, BMW's R90S was
not the fastest superbike of the mid-
1970s. Nor was it the quickest around a
racetrack; at least, not often. But for a rider with a
long distance to travel on straight roads and twisty
ones, there was nothing on two wheels that would
prove faster or more comfortable than the uniquely
well-equipped flat twin.

The BMW's distinctive smoked paint scheme
was perfectly in keeping with its image as a uniquely
refined and expensive sports-tourer. In many
respects, the R90S was the best all-round superbike
of its day. Certainly, no other production machine
could match its combination of 125mph (201km/h)
top speed, relaxed high-speed cruising ability, fine
handling, reliability and impeccable finish.

BMW had plenty of practice in building
horizontally opposed twins, and it showed. The
R90S came from a line of flat twins stretching back
to Max Fritz's original R32 of 1923. The German
firm had been building competent, comfortable and
conservative tourers for many years. But this bike,
shaped by noted stylist Hans Muth, had a distinctly
more aggressive personality.

The basics were typical BMW. Like the naked
R90/6, which was launched at the same time in
1973, the R90S owed much to the previous year's
R75. Enlarging the 745cc R75's bore from 82 to
90mm while retaining the 70.6mm stroke increased
capacity to 898cc. BMW also made a few other
updates, including a revised gearchange
mechanism, more powerful 280W alternator and
stronger bottom end.

There was more to the S-bike than just its fairing.
The engine was given a higher compression ratio,
9.5:1 against the 9:1 of the R90/6, and breathed in
through big 38mm Dell'Orto carbs with accelerator
pumps. Maximum power was 67bhp at 7000rpm,
an increase of 7bhp over the standard model. The
R90S also had a steering damper in its cockpit, a
larger fuel tank and a second front brake disc.

The extra power gave the S model a worthwhile
boost at high revs, without hindering either its
torquey mid-range response or its smoothness at
most engine speeds. Better still, the fairing meant
the engine's performance could be fully exploited
by the rider, who was free of the wind-blast

generated by every rival superbike. Other manufacturers would soon follow BMW's lead, but for the moment the fairing put the R90S in a class of its own.

Comfortable ride

Handling was good, too, despite suspension that was soft enough to give a comfortable ride. Despite its steering damper the S sometimes felt slightly light at the front when approaching its top speed, but that was even more true of most naked rivals. The twin-disc front brake system was reliable but lacked feel until uprated in 1975. Neat touches included a dashboard clock, generous fuel range of 200 miles (322km) or more, and a seat that allowed the rider to cover that distance in comfort.

BMWs had never been cheap, and the R90S, with its all-inclusive specification, was no exception to this rule. In many markets it was more than twice the price of Honda's CB750. That ensured the R90S would be ridden only by a select band of riders. Although the bike was a success, it was outsold by the standard 90/5.

Those riders fortunate enough to cover serious distance on the R90S knew that it was a very special motorcycle. If what you needed was a speed, handling ability and comfort, the R90S delivered in style. Oh, and sometimes it was the

Specification	BMW R90S (1974)
Engine	Air-cooled ohv four-valve pushrod flat twin
Capacity	898cc (90 x 70.6mm)
Maximum power	67bhp @ 7000rpm
Transmission	Five-speed, shaft final drive
Frame	Steel twin downtube
Suspension	Telescopic front; twin shocks rear
Brakes	Twin discs front; single disc rear
Weight	474lb (215kg) wet
Top speed	125mph (201km/h)

quickest superbike round a racetrack, too. BMW ace Reg Pridmore's victory in the 1976 US Superbike championship was proof of that.

Above: At heart the R90S was a traditional BMW boxer, but its fairing and especially its bold smoked grey or orange paint schemes gave a much more modern and attractive look. The bike's performance was backed by typically practical features including gaitered forks, a generous dual seat and shaft final drive.

Left: Although the R90S chassis was built for comfort as much as speed, the bike's rigid frame and fairly well-controlled suspension gave reliable handling. On long journeys, especially, few contemporary superbikes could match the effortless performance of BMW's flagship, which unfortunately had a hefty price tag to match its impressive specification.

Ducati 900SS

**Top speed
135mph**
217km/h

*Right: The Ducati's fairing
and slim build gave good
aerodynamics, which
combined with the twin's
light weight to make it
competitive against more
powerful rivals.*

*Below: Few bikes come
close to matching the
aggressive look of the
900SS, with its clip-on bars,
single seat and rearset
footrests, plus the desmo
V-twin engine's unfiltered
Dell'Orto carbs and free-
breathing Conti pipes.*

Ducati's original 900 Super Sport was one
of the most singleminded sporting
superbikes that ever devoured an innocent
public road. It was essentially a street-legal
production racer: fast, raw and uncompromising. It
handled and stopped brilliantly, looked and
sounded gorgeous and was a match for anything on
road or track.

The 900SS owed its existence to Ducati's
victory in the Imola 200 race in 1972, when factory
pilots Paul Smart and Bruno Spaggiari had finished
first and second ahead of numerous factory
opponents. The factory celebrated by producing a
small batch of road-legal replicas of the racebike.
These were popular, so more were built, this time
called the 750 Super Sport instead of Imola Replica
as the model had initially been known.

The half-faired 750SS mimicked Smart's fully
faired racer with its silver finish. Its 748cc V-twin
engine came from the firm's 750 Sport, and was
tuned with desmodromic valve operation, high-
compression forged pistons, polished internals, big
Dell'Orto carbs and free-breathing Conti pipes.

Fabio Taglioni's engine format of 90-degree, inline
V-twin with bevel drive to single overhead
camshafts had already become a Ducati trademark,
but this was the first roadgoing twin to use his
desmodromic system of positive valve closure.

Racing success

Ducati built only about 200 bikes, but all were snapped up and some were raced with good results in 1974. The Bologna factory was encouraged, and the following year created the more widely available 900SS, by replacing the smaller engine with a V-twin unit based on that of the existing 860GT. This combined a bigger, 86mm bore with the original 74.4mm stroke, giving a capacity of 864cc. Like the smaller model, it featured desmo valvegear, polished conrods, unfiltered 40mm Dell'Ortos and barely silenced Contis.

Those mods lifted peak power to an impressive 79bhp at 7000rpm at the crankshaft, or 68bhp at the rear wheel, and the 900SS had the chassis to match. Like its 750SS predecessor it was starkly functional, with its half-fairing, clip-on handlebars, rearset footrests, twin drilled Brembo front discs, and racy single seat. There was no electric starter, nor anything else not required for the bike's sole purpose of providing high performance.

The 900SS roared to a top speed of 135mph (217km/h), and cruised at 100mph (161km/h) with a smooth, long-legged feel. That was seriously fast in 1975, and the Ducati's handling was even better. It was not the most agile of bikes, but no rival could match the cornering poise and high-speed

Just Like Mike's – The Hailwood Replica

Paul Smart's Imola 200 win of 1972 was one great moment in Ducati's history, and another came six years later when Mike Hailwood, returning to racing from retirement, won the Isle of Man Formula One TT on a Ducati V-twin prepared by Sports Motorcycles. The following year Ducati introduced a special 900SS Hailwood Replica in honour of the victory. As well as a full fairing in Hailwood's red and green paint scheme, it featured gold-anodized Brembo brake calipers, new cast wheels and longer rear shocks. The Replica immediately became a bestseller, and remained in Ducati's range, with various modifications along the way, right up until 1985.

stability provided by the lean V-twin's blend of rigid frame, long wheelbase and taut Marzocchi suspension. Roadholding, braking and ground clearance were all exemplary too.

The uncompromising 900SS demanded commitment from it rider, and was too extreme for some. But it made a superb production racer. And for road riders who were captivated by its beauty, speed and pure-bred character, there was no bike to touch it. To paraphrase a road test of the time, the 900SS was a distillation of all the thrills and sensations that made high-performance motorcycling worthwhile.

Left: Ducati's 846cc, 90-degree V-twin engine featured bevel-shaft drive to its sohc, desmodromic valvegear. Long-legged power delivery and unshakeable high-speed stability were the 900SS trademarks.

Specification	Ducati 900SS (1975)
Engine	Air-cooled sohc four-valve 90-degree V-twin
Capacity	864cc (86 x 74.4mm)
Maximum power	79bhp at 7000rpm
Transmission	Five-speed, chain final drive
Frame	Steel ladder
Suspension	Telescopic front; twin shocks rear
Brakes	Twin discs front; single disc rear
Weight	414lb (188kg) wet
Top speed	135mph (217km/h)

Moto Guzzi Le Mans

**Top speed
130mph**
209km/h

*Above right: The Le Mans'
top speed of about 130mph
(209km/h) made it one of
the fastest bikes on the road
in the mid-1970s, and that
performance was delivered
with a relaxed feel that
encouraged fast cruising.
So too did the Guzzi's
excellent high-speed
handling, aided by firm and
well-damped suspension.*

*Below: Essentially the Le
Mans look was similar to
that of previous sporting
Guzzis. But the addition of
a bikini fairing, plus a new
dual seat whose front
section covered the rear of
the fuel tank, combined with
the Italian firm's trademark
engine layout to produce
one of the most glamorous
and distinctive of superbikes.*

 Long, lean and unmistakable, with its tiny headlamp fairing and muscular transverse V-twin engine, the Le Mans was arguably the most stylish superbike of the mid-1970s. Much more than that, it was fast, handled superbly and had excellent brakes. Guzzi's flagship was a hard-charging roadburner that could cruise effortlessly at 100mph (161km/h), carve through corners at a rapid pace, and generally keep up with the best of its rivals from Italy or Japan.

Moto Guzzi, based on the banks of Lake Como, had a long history of racing success and innovative bikes including the exotic 500cc V8 racer of the 1950s. Although still best known for its long-running singles, Guzzi was having increasing success with its distinctive transverse V-twins. But it was the Le Mans, introduced in 1976, that put the old firm back in the spotlight.

The Le Mans was based on the 750 S3, itself a striking and deceptively rapid unfaired roadster that had been developed from the earlier V7 Sport, Guzzi's first high-performance V-twin. The new bike's most obvious innovation was its striking styling, which combined the headlamp fairing with a curvaceous fuel tank and angular seat.

In search of more power, Guzzi enlarged the S3's 748cc engine to 844cc, and increased compression ratio from 9.8:1 to 10.2:1. They also fitted unfiltered 36mm Dell'Orto carburettors plus a new, free-breathing exhaust system. The shaft-drive V-twin was still a fairly old-fashioned device with pushrod valve operation and a slow-shifting five-speed gearbox. But it now produced 80bhp at

7300rpm, an increase of 8bhp, and had plenty of mid-range punch, which the smaller S3 motor had rather disappointingly lacked.

That extra power was enough for a top speed of 130mph (209km/h), impressive at the time. The big motor was lumpy at low speed, but smoothed out as the revs rose, and pulled hard through the mid-range. Where the Guzzi really scored was with its uniquely long-legged feel which, in combination with the leant-forward riding position and protection from the flyscreen, enabled the Le Mans' rider to keep up those speeds for long periods without discomfort.

Fine handling

A rigid steel frame gave fine handling despite the occasionally unsettling effect of the shaft final drive. The Le Mans wasn't the lightest or most manoeuvrable of bikes but its high-speed stability was immense, thanks partly to typically stiff suspension. At speeds that would have the riders of rival Japanese superbikes weaving, the Guzzi rumbled on without a twitch, its rider tucked down at the clip-ons behind that neat flyscreen.

Guzzi's brake set-up of three linked, cast iron Brembo discs was far superior to most rival systems, too, especially in the wet. The handlebar lever operated one front disc; the foot pedal the other plus the rear. By Italian standards the Guzzi was well built and reliable, too, although it suffered from typically poor electrics.

The Le Mans' high price ensured that it was never going to sell in huge numbers, but it gained a cult following, opened many riders' eyes to Guzzi's quirky V-twins, and remained in production for 19 years, through a series of updates. Unfortunately its performance did not improve with age.

On the contrary, the Le Mans Mk2 version of 1979 was slightly slower, though it at least gave its rider the benefit of an angular full fairing. The 1982 model Mk3 regained some power, but Guzzi made things worse in 1985 with the 949cc Le Mans Mk4, whose 16-inch front wheel gave unreliable handling. By this time, the stability and competitive speed of the 1976 model were just a fond memory. In the case of the Moto Guzzi Le Mans, original was definitely best.

Specification	Moto Guzzi Le Mans 850 (1976)
Engine	Air-cooled ohv four-valve pushrod 90-degree transverse V-twin
Capacity	844cc (83 x 78mm)
Maximum power	80bhp at 7300rpm
Transmission	Five-speed, shaft final drive
Frame	Steel spine
Suspension	Telescopic front; twin shocks rear
Brakes	Twin discs front; single disc rear
Weight	476lb (216kg) wet
Top speed	130mph (209km/h)

Laverda Jota

**Top speed
140mph**
225km/h

*Below: The Jota's great
asset was engine
performance rather than
handling, but the big
Laverda cornered well
enough to keep it ahead of
its rivals on road and track.
Firm suspension helped
maintain stability in most
situations, despite the
combined effect of the
triple's size, weight and
sheer brute horsepower.*

There was no mistaking the appeal of the Laverda Jota. The Italian triple backed up its square-jawed naked style with massive, sometimes intimidating, performance. The Jota was big, brutal, loud and supremely powerful. In the right hands it was simply the fastest thing on two wheels in the late 1970s, as a string of production race victories confirmed.

This most famous of Laverda's 981cc air-cooled triples resulted from a collaboration between the firm from Breganze in northern Italy and Slater Brothers, its British importer. The basis of the Jota was the 3C, itself a potent and handsome machine, which Laverda had created in 1973, essentially by adding an extra cylinder to its existing 650cc parallel twin.

In 1975 brothers Roger and Richard Slater, intending to production race the triple, created a machine they called the 3CE – the 'E' standing for England – by fitting modifications including a free-breathing exhaust system, rearset footrests and

single seat. Meanwhile the factory was developing its own update, the 3CL, which featured cast wheels, triple disc brakes and a tail fairing, and was introduced as a 1976 model.

Combining the two bikes created the machine that the Slaters christened the Jota, after a Spanish dance in three-four time. This time they went further with the engine tuning, fitting the dohc triple with factory endurance race camshafts and high-compression pistons. The result was a substantially increased peak output of 90bhp at 8000rpm, with noise and performance to match.

This was an Italian bike that could live with Japan's finest for sheer horsepower and speed. The Jota felt rough below about 4000rpm due to its lumpy cams, but came alive above that figure with exhilarating acceleration, a soulful three-cylinder bellow and a top speed of 140mph (225km/h).

The triple was a demanding bike to ride, its power delivery and sheer speed combining with the unfaired riding position, engine vibration and a

Mirage – The Fast-Touring Triple

Laverda produced another fine superbike in 1978 by enlarging the 981cc engine to 1116cc, and fitting higher handlebars plus a larger dual seat to create a slightly softer, touring-oriented model called the 1200. Again, Slater Brothers uprated it with hot cams and a free-breathing exhaust system (compression ratio was left standard) to produce the Mirage. The result was a fast, yet very torquey and versatile, machine. The Laverda factory adopted the Mirage name, although for most markets the bike retained its standard cams and exhaust.

heavy clutch to make the rider work hard. In other respects the Laverda was well-equipped, with finish and electrics that were excellent by Italian standards. Handling was generally good, thanks to a strong frame and typically firm Ceriani suspension. But the triple was a tall, heavy machine that required plenty of muscle from its rider, and was prone to weave at high speed. The trio of big, cast iron Brembo discs gave plenty of stopping power, wet or dry.

Obvious appeal

Although the Jota was assembled in Breganze (apart from silencers and collector box), the tuned triple was officially a UK-only model. But limited numbers were sold in other markets including America. The price was high, but the appeal was obvious: this was arguably the world's fastest roadster in 1976. Slaters' racer Peter Davies supported that claim by dominating the British production race championship.

Laverda modified the triple in subsequent years, notably with a variety of half-fairings, and in 1982 produced a more refined version, the Jota 120. This had a 120-degree firing order, in place of the old 180-degree (one piston up, two down) arrangement. The Jota 120 was much smoother, yet retained the traditional triple character. Although short-lived, it was a fine way to end the famous line.

Below left: Laverda's 981cc dohc triple was a potent unit in standard form, and became even more impressive when tuned to Jota specification with factory endurance racing camshafts, plus pistons that raised compression ratio from 9:1 to 10:1. The result was a peak output of 90bhp.

Below: The Jota's raw, muscular styling was always a big part of its appeal. This bike has the classical early combination of low-set adjustable handlebars, humped seat and Laverda's traditional orange paintwork. In the 1980s the triple could be bought with an optional half-fairing that made high-speed cruising a more practical proposition.

Specification	Laverda Jota (1976)
Engine	Air-cooled dohc six-valve triple
Capacity	981cc (75 x 74mm)
Maximum power	90bhp at 8000rpm
Transmission	Five-speed, chain final drive
Frame	Steel twin downtube
Suspension	Telescopic front; twin shocks rear
Brakes	Twin discs front; single disc rear
Weight	521lb (236kg) wet
Top speed	140mph (225km/h)

Suzuki GS1000

**Top speed
135mph**
217km/h

*Below: Suzuki's big four
was a good-looking
machine whose style was
very similar to that of the
GS750 and 550 models,
both of which had been
launched one year earlier
in 1977.*

 At first sight Suzuki's GS1000 was an unlikely bike to be regarded as outstanding; let alone as a machine that would be regarded as an all-time great even decades after its arrival in 1978. Although pleasantly styled, the GS was unexceptional to look at. Its air-cooled, dohc four-cylinder engine design was entirely conventional, as was its steel-framed, twin-shock chassis layout.

But the GS1000 *was* extra special, for two main reasons. Firstly, it was slightly better in just about every quantifiable way than its direct rival, Kawasaki's Z1000 – meaning that Suzuki's first ever open-class machine was the best big four on the road. More importantly, the GS could be ridden extremely hard without wobbles or weaves, which arguably made it the first Japanese superbike to match European levels of chassis performance.

Stability and cornering prowess

Coming as it did towards the end of a decade in which Japanese machines had gradually assumed dominance due to their powerful and reliable engines, without managing to shake off criticisms of second-rate chassis, the Suzuki's arrival was significant. Here at last was a bike that was not only faster than any other four in a straight line, but whose stability and cornering prowess allowed – no, positively encouraged – its rider to make the most of all that power.

Specification	Suzuki GS1000 (1978)
Engine	Air-cooled dohc eight-valve four
Capacity	997cc (70 x 64.8mm)
Maximum power	87bhp @ 8000rpm
Transmission	Five-speed, chain final drive
Frame	Steel twin downtube
Suspension	Telescopic front; twin shocks rear
Brakes	Twin discs front; disc rear
Weight	533lb (242kg) wet
Top speed	135mph (217km/h)

The achievement of Suzuki's engineers was all the greater given that the firm's first four-stroke multi, the excellent GS750, had itself been launched only one year earlier. The larger powerplant, which had a capacity of 997cc from dimensions of 70 x 64.8mm, followed the 750's dohc eight-valve layout and actually weighed slightly less, due to features including a lighter flywheel, thinner crankcases and lack of a kick-starter. But the bigger motor was considerably more powerful, producing a maximum of 87bhp at 8000rpm that was 19bhp up on the GS750, and gave a 4bhp advantage over the Z1000.

The GS1000 shared its overall look and steel, twin-downtube frame layout with the GS750. But the new bike's frame was thicker in places, and its tubular steel swingarm was stronger. The GS1000 also had wider tyres, plus an extra front brake disc. Its new forks were air-assisted, and its shocks could be adjusted through four rebound damping positions – giving the GS the most sophisticated suspension system yet seen on a mass-produced roadster. (So it did have some technical innovation, after all.)

This added-up to a stunning new superbike that seemingly had no real weakness, and which made the Z1000, until now the dominant big four, look slightly second rate. The GS stormed past the 100mph (161km/h) mark at a phenomenal rate, on the way to a top speed of 135mph (217km/h). Cruising speed was limited only by road conditions and the rider's ability to hang on. Even at high revs the motor felt unburstable and reasonably smooth, and it soon proved to be impressively reliable.

Better still, that chassis really was capable of keeping all that horsepower in check. One tester observed that the GS1000 felt safer at 110mph (177km/h) than most bikes did at less than half that speed. Although it was not a particularly light bike, its frame was rigid and its suspension was the best yet seen from Japan. Despite the bike's high-speed stability, it could be flicked into corners with the ease of a much smaller machine.

Considering that this was Suzuki's first attempt at a open-class superbike, the GS1000's overall performance was nothing short of sensational. Apart from a few minor criticisms such as the lack of a pillion grab-rail as standard fitment, the GS's only real failing was a slight lack of character. Given its speed, its reliability, and most of all its handling, very few riders complained about that.

Left: Round chromed caps at the ends of each camshaft distinguished the air-cooled, eight-valve GS1000 engine from the Kawasaki Z1000 unit that it closely resembled. Suzuki's engine was lighter as well as slightly more powerful, with a peak output of 87bhp.

Below: Handling was the most impressive yet from an open-class Japanese superbike, thanks mainly to the Suzuki's combination of rigid steel frame and superior suspension. The quality of the GS's air-assisted front forks and damping-adjustable rear shocks allowed the engine's power to be used to the full.

Honda CBX1000

**Top speed
135mph**
217km/h

Below: The CBX1000 had only two silencers, but even so the six-cylinder engine combined with neat styling to give the Honda a dramatic look from almost every angle. Compared to the large and muscular motor, the bike's thin front forks, narrow tyres and small brake discs seem insubstantial, although they were top class components in 1978.

Honda's mighty six-cylinder CBX1000 was the superbike that appeared to have it all. Its 24-valve engine produced a phenomenal 105bhp, making the CBX the most powerful production motorcycle on the road in 1978. Its searing speed was backed by remarkable smoothness and technical sophistication, even by Honda's high standards.

The Six was a handsome machine that had a pure-bred sporting image. It came with a sense of history, having been inspired by Honda's famous multi-cylinder racebikes of the mid-1960s. And its chassis was excellent, too, boosted by innovative use of weight-reducing materials.

Years after the bike's launch, it still inspires great loyalty from a devoted band of enthusiasts, and respect from most people who have ridden one. It remains a landmark machine, having combined style, technology and performance in a way arguably not seen before or since from Japan. Yet ironically the Six was a short-lived sales failure when new.

Multi-cylinder heritage

The CBX1000 was shaped by project leader Shoichiro Irimajiri, who as a young engineer in the 1960s had worked to create Honda's high-revving multi-cylinder grand prix bikes raced by Mike Hailwood, Luigi Taveri and others. The racers provided inspiration for the CBX's cylinder head, with its 24 tiny valves. The exhaust camshaft was hollow to save weight. The CBX trod new ground for a standard machine by using lightweight magnesium for several engine covers.

Irimajiri got round the potential width problem of a six-cylinder motor with a jackshaft, above the gearbox, which drove the alternator and ignition system. This allowed the 1047cc motor to be remarkably narrow at its base. Legroom was provided for the rider by tilting the cylinders forward by 33 degrees, and by angling the six carbs inwards in two pairs of three.

Honda created the CBX as a no-compromise sports bike. Its styling was dramatic, emphasized by the way in which the wide engine, which being

air-cooled required no radiator, was suspended by the tubular steel frame. The absence of downtubes added to the visual impact.

Straight-line performance was awesome, combining smoothness with the most ferocious acceleration yet seen from a production bike. Below 6000rpm the CBX responded crisply but without great force. Above that figure it came alive, surging towards its 135mph (217km/h) top-speed with a memorable, high-pitched howl from its exhaust. Most riders who rode the big six-cylinder machine were captivated by its unique blend of speed and charisma.

Its chassis worked, too. The CBX had good quality suspension, plus an efficient twin-disc front brake. Weight was kept to a minimum by use of aluminium handlebars, plastic mudguards and magnesium engine covers. Although the Honda still weighed a substantial 572lb (259kg), and could not match the composure of Suzuki's new GS1000 four, it handled well for such a big bike.

But for all its pace and panache, the CBX sold very poorly, especially in the vital (and touring oriented) American market. Part of the reason was simply that the Six cost far more than its less exotic rivals. In some markets it was 50 per cent more expensive than equivalent fours, yet offered no real advantage in terms of pure performance.

After a 1981 redesign that created the fully-faired CBX1000B, an attempt to add appeal for long-distance riders, the Six was dropped from the range. Honda's gamble had failed. But the CBX had given the firm's image a considerable boost. As one star-struck tester had put it in 1978, 'the Six is one of those rare machines that will never, ever be forgotten.' As long as fast bikes are ridden and admired, there is absolutely no danger of that.

Left: The CBX frame had no front downtubes to spoil the dramatic view of the six-cylinder powerplant, fitted here with Honda's crash-bars. The 24-valve unit's 105bhp output gave fierce acceleration and was very smooth and reliable.

Specification	Honda CBX1000 (1978)
Engine	Air-cooled dohc 24-valve six
Capacity	1047cc (64.5 x 53.4mm)
Maximum power	105bhp @ 9000rpm
Transmission	Five-speed, chain final drive
Frame	Tubular steel
Suspension	Telescopic front; twin shocks rear
Brakes	Twin discs front; disc rear
Weight	572lb (259kg) wet
Top speed	135mph (217km/h)

Left: Despite innovative use of lightweight materials such as aluminium, plastic and magnesium, the CBX was a heavy machine. But considering its size it handled well, partly because Honda had designed it very much as a sports bike, with reasonably firm suspension. The engine was even quite narrow at its base, giving good cornering clearance.

Honda CB1100R

**Top speed
142mph**
229km/h

*Below: The original, 1981-
model CB1100R had a half-
fairing plus other features
designed for long-distance
production racing,
including a large-capacity
fuel tank and single seat.
Other key elements were its
twin-piston front brake
calipers, remote-reservoir
rear shocks, and the tuned
and strengthened 1062cc
four-cylinder engine with
its unmatched 115bhp
power output.*

The incomparable CB1100R provided proof that when mighty Honda set out to build the fastest production motorcycle in the world, the opposition didn't stand much chance. Especially when the bike in question was a purpose-built racer designed with little regard to cost, produced in very small numbers, and which competed against mass-produced machines that sold for half its price.

Honda's aim in creating the CB1100R was victory in high-profile long-distance production races in Australia (especially the prestigious Castrol Six Hour) and South Africa. Regulations for these races were strict, with very few modifications allowed. So Honda created its first 'homologation special' by treating its current top model, the naked CB900FZ, to a spectacular makeover.

The result was a stunning superbike that was head and shoulders above all opposition in 1981. Its racetrack dominance was predictable and sometimes dull. But for the fortunate few who got to ride an 1100R, there was nothing remotely boring about a bike that rocketed to over 140mph (225km/h), handled and braked better than any big

four-cylinder rival, and was even refined and comfortable too.

Honda's first requirement was more power. The CB900's air-cooled, 16-valve four-cylinder motor was bored out to increase its capacity from 901 to 1062cc, and its compression ratio raised from 8.8 to 10:1. That lifted peak output by more than 20 per cent, to 115bhp at 9000rpm. Equally importantly, the motor was strengthened with modifications including new conrods, wider primary chain and redesigned crankcases.

Chassis layout remained conventional, but the 1100R benefited from a more rigid twin-downtube steel frame, plus the most sophisticated cycle parts yet seen on a production motorcycle. Front forks had thick 37mm legs and adjustable air pressure, while the shocks could be fine-tuned for compression and rebound damping, and had the novel feature of remote hydraulic reservoirs, to resist overheating. The front brake held another first, with its twin-piston calipers.

One thing that Honda didn't achieve was make the CB1100R particularly light: at 518lb (235kg) dry, it was slightly heavier the 900FZ despite much

use of plastic and aluminium. The production racer certainly looked the part, though, with its half-fairing, large fuel tank (for maximum racing range), and racy single seat. Nobody was in the slightest doubt about why the 1100R had been created, especially when Honda announced that only 1000 units would be built, and that in some markets the bike would cost almost twice as much as the CB900FZ.

Nothing this purposeful had been produced by a Japanese manufacturer before, and the 1100R duly trounced all opposition on the track. This was particularly true in the shorter races of the British Streetbike series, where the handful of Hondas were in a race of their own at the head of the field. The southern hemisphere long-distance events threw up more variables, but the CB1100R took plenty of wins.

Sensational road bike

Perhaps most impressively of all, the CB1100R made a sensational road bike. Its phenomenal top-end power was matched not only by storming mid-range acceleration, but also by impressive smoothness and low-rev refinement. The protective fairing allowed more of that performance to be used. And although the 1100R was prone to a slight weave at very high speed, its chassis gave superb suspension control, fierce braking and generous ground clearance.

Honda made the bike even better in the next couple of years. In 1982 came the CB1100R-C, with a full fairing (which cured the instability), dual seat, improved front forks and wider wheels.

Specification	Honda CB1100R (1981)
Engine	Air-cooled dohc 16-valve four
Capacity	1062cc (70 x 69mm)
Maximum power	115bhp @ 9000rpm
Transmission	Five-speed, chain final drive
Frame	Steel twin downtube
Suspension	Telescopic front; twin shocks rear
Brakes	Twin discs front; disc rear
Weight	518lb (235kg) dry
Top speed	142mph (229km/h)

A year later, the 1100R-D added damping-adjustable forks and an aluminium swingarm. The specification had changed, but one thing had not: the CB1100R was still the fastest production motorcycle in the world.

Above: As well as being an almost invincible production racer, the CB1100R made a superb roadster. This is the later, fully-faired model, pictured on the Isle of Man during TT week. If there had been a Production TT race in the early 1980s, the CB1100R would doubtless have won that too.

Left: Joey Dunlop rode the CB1100R to some good results in the British production-based Streetbike championship in 1981. The Honda dominated and Ron Haslam won all but the final round, where he was beaten into second place by another future grand prix star, Wayne Gardner – also on a CB1100R.

Suzuki Katana 1100

**Top speed
140mph**
225km/h

The Katana 1100 that Suzuki unleashed on an unsuspecting motorcycle world in 1982 was a machine like nothing seen before from Japan. It was bold, stylish, imaginative, breathtaking; very different to the succession of fast but visually dull models that had preceded it. And underneath all the fancy bodywork, the Katana was an outstanding superbike too.

Katana was the Japanese word for a Samurai warrior's ceremonial sword, and it fitted Suzuki's sharp new silver blade perfectly. With its pointed nose, tiny flyscreen, low clip-on handlebars and swooping tank-seat section, the Katana was a unique machine with an infinitely more aggressive image than the GSX1100 roadster to which it was closely related.

This landmark in the history of Japanese superbike development had partly European parentage. The Katana had been shaped by the German group Target Design (which had also been responsible for BMW's striking R90S almost a decade earlier). Although some riders criticized the Suzuki for being more notable for style than practicality, most welcomed the alternative to the

formatted 'Universal Japanese Motorcycle' with its four-cylinder engine and unfaired, upright riding position that provided no wind protection.

Suzuki had the ideal basis for the Katana in the 1075cc air-cooled engine from the GSX1100, with its 16 valves, phenomenally broad spread of power, and reputation for reliability. To give the new bike extra teeth, the motor was tuned with a modified airbox, reworked carburettors, new exhaust camshaft and lightened alternator. It produced a maximum of 111bhp at 8500rpm, a useful 11bhp up on the standard unit.

Chassis layout remained conventional, and the twin-cradle steel frame was unchanged, but many parts were new. Suspension was stiffened at both ends, new triple clamps gave a shallower steering angle for added stability, and the front forks gained a hydraulic anti-dive system claimed to be similar to that of Suzuki's 500cc grand prix racers.

Breathtaking acceleration

The Katana looked lightning fast when standing still, and when moving it was much, much faster. The big GSX motor was already a superb

Below: The Katana's sleek and integrated style was a welcome departure following years of Japanese multis with conventional look and riding position. Although the nose fairing and tiny screen gave minimal wind protection, they combined with the fairly low handlebars to improve high-speed comfort. This bike's four-into-one exhaust and remote-reservoir shocks are later additions.

Left: Firm suspension and an anti-dive front suspension system, developed from the one fitted to Suzuki's grand prix racebikes, helped give the big Katana excellent handling by Japanese superbike standards. Sticky tyres and generous ground clearance encouraged enthusiastic cornering provided the road was dry.

powerplant, with huge reserves of instant mid-range torque. The Katana had breathtaking acceleration – and even more urge at the top end. Top speed was a genuine 140mph (225km/h). And the Katana's stretched-forward riding position, with its welcome bit of wind protection from the small screen, made that performance more usable than that of most rivals.

Handling was very good for such a big, heavy bike. The fairing and screen were solidly mounted, so contributing to the Katana's impressive high-speed stability. The firm suspension gave a level of control (and discomfort) that was almost Italian, marred only by the anti-dive's occasional tendency to make the forks lock up over a series of bumps. The triple-disc brake system worked well, even in the wet, though this could not be said of the standard fitment tyres.

Inevitably, the radical Katana did not suit every rider or every occasion. Its suspension was harsh and uncomfortable in town, its seat was hard, and its steering was quite heavy at slow speed. But this was not a bike to be ridden at slow speed. Its

purposeful nature was an integral part of its appeal. At last, this was a Japanese bike that provided both performance, handling and style, at a sensible price.

The Katana was a huge hit, and remained popular for years. Suzuki broadened the Katana range with a 1000cc version with slide carbs for production racing, watered-down middleweight models, and even pocket-sized 250 and 400cc replicas for the Japanese market. Years later they even restarted production of a 'special edition' Katana 1100 that was almost identical to the original. Fair reward for a brave and brilliant bike.

Above: Suzuki's 1075cc, air-cooled, 16-valve engine had been introduced with the conventionally styled GSX1100 in 1980, two years before the Katana's arrival. Its four-valves-per-cylinder layout, called TSCC (or Twin Swirl Combustion Chamber) by Suzuki, gave superbly strong mid-range output.

Specification	Suzuki GSX1100S Katana (1982)
Engine	Air-cooled dohc 16-valve four
Capacity	1075cc (72 x 66mm)
Maximum power	111bhp @ 8500rpm
Transmission	Five-speed, chain final drive
Frame	Steel twin downtube
Suspension	Telescopic front; twin shocks rear
Brakes	Twin discs front; disc rear
Weight	545lb (247kg) wet
Top speed	140mph (225km/h)

Kawasaki GPZ900R

**Top speed
155mph**
249km/h

*Below: The Ninja's
aerodynamic full fairing
and compact dimensions
helped give the 908cc bike
a top speed of over 150mph
(241km/h). The original
bike's 16-inch front wheel
was changed to a wider 17-
inch unit on later models.*

The GPZ900R was the machine with
which Kawasaki recaptured its reputation
for unbeatable four-cylinder performance.
When the firm's first liquid-cooled four stormed
onto the streets in 1984, the manner in which it
delivered 150mph (241km/h) top speed with
smoothness and unprecedented refinement
confirmed that a thrilling new era had begun.

And there was much more than sheer speed to
the bike that in most markets was known as the
Ninja. This was a 908cc machine that felt as
compact as a 750 – and which outran its 1100cc
rivals when you opened the throttle. Street riders
took to it in droves, production racers adopted it as
their own. Almost everyone who rode the Ninja
was won over by a machine that combined speed

with reliability, handling, comfort and its own
unmistakable style.

Kawasaki had spent the previous decade
earning a reputation for brilliant air-cooled eight-
valve motors, but the GPZ unit was distinctly
different. As well as liquid-cooling, it featured a
16-valve cylinder head plus developments
including a balancer shaft, camchain at the end of
the crankshaft, and alternator above the six-speed
gearbox. It was small, light and powerful, though
its peak output of 113bhp at 9500rpm was slightly
below that of the old GPz1100.

The rest of the GPZ maintained the theme of
high performance with minimum size and weight.
Kawasaki called the bike's frame layout a
'diamond' but essentially it was a steel spine design

that used the engine as a stressed member, and which dispensed with the conventional downtubes. Aluminium was used for the square-section rear subframe, the box-section swingarm, and the large alloy footrest hangers on which it pivoted.

Front forks were 38mm units incorporating an anti-dive system that increased compression damping with suspension travel. Rear suspension was by Kawasaki's Uni-Trak monoshock layout, with an air-assisted shock unit that could be adjusted for rebound damping. The front wheel was 16 inches in diameter, following the fashion of the day.

Searing speed

The sharply styled full fairing did a reasonable job of shielding the rider, who leant forward to fairly flat handlebars. The Ninja was low, sleek – and most of all it was fast. Due to its superior aerodynamics it had a top-speed edge over its GPz1100 predecessor, with dramatic acceleration above 6000rpm and searing speed from 8000rpm to the 10,500rpm redline.

And the rest of the bike did not let it down. High-speed stability was exemplary, partly due to suspension that gave a superbly taut feel at the expense of some harshness at slower speeds. At over 500lb (227kg) the 900 was no lightweight, but by superbike standards it was very manageable, and its twin front disc brakes were hugely powerful. The Kawasaki was also practical, combining a generous fuel range with reasonable comfort plus neat details including luggage hooks and a strong pillion grab-rail.

The Ninja's success when launched was predictable, but even Kawasaki must have been pleasantly surprised by its long life. The 900 outlasted its intended replacements, the GPZ1000RX and the ZX-10, and even in 1990 was

not replaced but merely updated. The front wheel grew from 16 to 17 inches in diameter; both wheels were widened to allow fitment of fatter tyres; forks were thickened to 41mm; and front brake discs were enlarged to 300mm and treated to new four-piston calipers.

As it remained in Kawasaki's range during the 1990s, the once mighty Ninja came to be regarded as a budget-priced sports-tourer rather than a serious high-performance machine. But that should not diminish its reputation. What should be remembered is that in 1984 the GPZ900R was the undisputed king of the road. And that it started the dynasty of liquid-cooled, 16-valve Kawasaki fours that continues to this day.

Specification	Kawasaki GPZ900R (1984)
Engine	Liquid-cooled dohc 16-valve four
Capacity	908cc (72.5 x 55mm)
Maximum power	113bhp @ 9500rpm
Transmission	Six-speed, chain final drive
Frame	Steel spine
Suspension	Telescopic front; single shock rear
Brakes	Twin discs front; disc rear
Weight	502lb (228kg) dry
Top speed	155mph (249km/h)

Yamaha V-Max

**Top speed
140mph**
225km/h

*Right: High speed on the
V-Max was great fun,
provided you were travelling
in a straight line. Corners
were a different matter.*

*Below: In a contest to find
the ultimate production
musclebike, there would be
only one contender. The
aggressive, engine-
dominated styling would
barely change in almost two
decades of production.*

 There has never been a production
motorcycle like the V-Max. Nor has there
been a modern high-performance bike that
has remained successful with so few changes as
Yamaha's intimidating and brutally powerful V4,
which was unleashed on an unsuspecting public
back in 1985.

On its introduction, the V-Max's muscular
styling and its 1198cc engine's 143bhp output put it
in a different league to every other bike on the
road. It was designed by Americans and resembled
a two-wheeled muscle car, with big alloy air-scoops
jutting out from the side of its dummy fuel tank.
The scoops and tank were fake but the V-Max's
performance was certainly not. Nothing wrenched
your arms like the Max. The fact that its chassis
was barely able to cope simply added to the impact.

The undoubted centrepiece of the V-Max was
its engine, a 72-degree, shaft-drive V4 borrowed
from the Venture tourer. Yamaha's engineers tuned
the Venture's 95bhp, 16-valve engine with
conventional hot-rodding components including
high-lift cams, big valves, lightened pistons and a
toughened crankshaft. They also added V-boost, a
system that linked the carburettors to provide extra
mixture – and instant extra power – at high revs.

Storming acceleration

The effect of snapping open the throttle was breathtaking. When the needle of the Yamaha's tiny tachometer hit 6000rpm, the V-boost cut in to send the bike hurtling in a barely controlled frenzy towards the horizon. Other bikes were ultimately faster than the Yamaha, whose aerodynamics limited top speed to 140mph (225km/h). But nothing could live with the V-Max away from the line. It stormed off, painting a black stripe on the ground with its wildly spinning rear tyre, which at 150 x 15in was motorcycling's widest.

Cornering was often equally exciting, and not always for the right reasons. The Yamaha carried its weight low (fuel lived under the seat, which helped), but there was no disguising the fact that this was one heavy, fairly crudely suspended motorbike that didn't much like changing direction. At moderate cornering speeds it was stable, but more aggressive riding resulted in the big Yamaha shaking its head in annoyance.

Not that most owners seemed to mind, for part of the V-Max's uniquely macho appeal was that it had too much motor for its chassis. In an era of increasingly sweet-handling superbikes it stood out

Egli's Madder Max

The V-Max's power and aggressive image made it an ideal base for tuners and specials builders, who have used it as the basis of many outstanding creations over the years. Among the most outrageous was the supercharged monster built by veteran Swiss engineer Fritz Egli in 1995. Egli bolted on a Roots supercharger, driven by toothed belt from the crankshaft, and fed by a gaping twin-choke Weber carburettor in the dummy fuel tank. The result was over 200bhp, ear-splitting noise, and performance that was terrifying despite the mildly uprated chassis. Despite requests, Egli refused to build more bikes for sale.

as a mean, nasty machine that was unbeatable in a straight line but hard work through the bends. Yet it was also easy to live with, when required. That big V4 was docile at low revs, and also commendably reliable.

The V-Max's unique style and performance earned it a cult following back in 1985 (although, ironically, it was initially detuned in some markets including Britain), and it remained in Yamaha's range for many years with few changes. In 1993 it gained thicker front forks and an uprated front brake. But the mighty Max entered its third decade with its essential look and personality barely changed at all. And with its reputation for raw, brutal power very much in place.

Left: The air-scoops sticking out above each side of the engine were fake, and the fuel tank was a dummy because fuel lived under the seat. But the big V4's engine performance, at least in unrestricted form, was the real thing. Front forks and brakes were uprated on later models, but there was no need to tune the 143bhp motor.

Specification	Yamaha V-Max (1985)
Engine	Liquid-cooled dohc 16-valve 72-degree V4
Capacity	1198cc (76 x 66mm)
Maximum power	143bhp @ 8000rpm
Transmission	Five-speed, shaft final drive
Frame	Steel twin downtube
Suspension	Telescopic front; twin shocks rear
Brakes	Twin discs front; disc rear
Weight	560lb (254kg) dry
Top speed	140mph (225km/h)

Suzuki GSX-R750

**Top speed
145mph**
233km/h

*Below: One glance
confirmed that the GSX-R
was the spitting image of
Suzuki's endurance race
bike, and the roadster's
power, light weight and
handling ability soon made
it a hit on road and track.
This is a 1986-model
GSX-R, featuring the longer
swingarm introduced to
improve high-speed stability.*

The original GSX-R750 was the bike with
which modern Japanese super-sports
motorcycles were invented. True, there
had been plenty of fast and fiery superbikes before
the oil-cooled four was unleashed in 1985. But the
GSX-R750 was the first modern race replica; a
uniquely single-minded machine built for
performance above all else.

Its layout matched that of Suzuki's endurance
racers of the previous year, from the shape of the
twin-headlamp fairing to the use of 18-inch wheels
(favoured by endurance race teams because the
larger diameter facilitated brake pad changes)
instead of the then fashionable 16-inchers. Its frame
was made from aluminium, instead of the steel
used by rival superbikes. And its 749cc, dohc 16-
valve engine was powerful, with a peak output of
100bhp at 10,500rpm.

Oil cooling system

That output came from a motor that used the novel
(for bikes) system of oil-cooling to reduce cylinder
temperatures without the added bulk and weight of
a water jacket. The Suzuki Advanced Cooling
System, SACS for short, allowed the engineers to
redesign the previous air-cooled GSX750 unit on a
smaller, higher-revving scale. Almost every
component lost weight by being smaller or, in the
case of the cam cover, made from exotic
magnesium instead of aluminium.

The GSX-R motor's output and lightness were
impressive, but it was the chassis that did most to
give this bike its unmatched power-to-weight ratio.
At 388lb (176kg) the GSX-R was far lighter than
any rival 750. According to Suzuki, the new
aluminium frame, constructed from a combination
of cast sections and extruded tubes, weighed just

18lb (8kg), half as much as the GSX750's less rigid steel item. Front forks were stout 41mm units, their rigidity boosted by an aluminium brace.

A racy instrument console, with dials mounted in foam, hinted at the motor's liking for revs. Despite its row of Mikuni flat-slide carburettors the Suzuki was quite rideable even at low engine speed, feeling slightly buzzy without ever producing serious vibration. But its delivery was flat until 7000rpm, when the bike suddenly came alive, howling forward as the revs headed towards the 11,000rpm limit.

High-revving performance

That high-revving performance, allied to a slick six-speed gearbox and a top speed of 145mph (233km/h), made the GSX-R a straight-line match for all its 750cc rivals. And in the bends the Suzuki pressed home its advantage. Despite its 18-inch front wheel the bike could be flicked into a turn with little effort, and was stable once leant over. The GSX-R's lack of weight was a benefit in corners and under braking, where it allowed the front brake – a combination of 300mm discs and four-piston calipers – to deliver unprecedented stopping power and feel.

But the GSX-R was one of the first road bikes to require careful setting-up, and preferably a steering damper, to handle well. The original model's occasional high-speed wobble prompted Suzuki to introduce a slightly longer swingarm in 1986. Practicality had barely been a consideration for the Suzuki's designers, but the GSX-R750 did have a protective fairing and a strong pillion grab-rail, to offset against its aggressive riding position, poor fuel range and narrow mirrors.

Specification	Suzuki GSX-R750 (1985)
Engine	Oil-cooled dohc 16-valve four
Capacity	749cc (70 x 48.7mm)
Maximum power	100bhp @ 10,500rpm
Transmission	Six-speed, chain final drive
Frame	Aluminium twin downtube
Suspension	Telescopic front; single shock rear
Brakes	Twin discs front; disc rear
Weight	388lb (176kg) dry
Top speed	145mph (233km/h)

Not that many riders who bought GSX-R750s for use on road or track were concerned about such details. The GSX-R was built for speed, and it delivered. It became hugely popular, was repeatedly updated in subsequent years (not always successfully), and established a race replica format that would be followed by Suzuki and its rival firms into the 21st century.

Below: Whether carving through turns or flat-out on a straight, the GSX-R was a fast and exciting ride. Its light yet rigid aluminium frame (bottom left) heralded a new era in sports bike chassis design.

Honda RC30

**Top speed
155mph**
249km/h

*Below: Behind the RC30's
compact twin-headlamp
fairing, which was closely
based on that of the RVF
racebike, were the two
elaborately constructed
curved radiators necessary
to cool the powerful V4
engine. The Honda's front
brake and multi-adjustable
front forks were the best yet
seen on a streetbike.*

The concept of the race replica was firmly
established when Honda launched its
RC30 in 1988, but there had never been a
superbike remotely like this. With its exotic
specification, its race-bred V4 engine and its high
price, the bike officially known as the VFR750R
was a direct descendant of Honda's mighty
RVF750 works machines, which had dominated
world championship Formula One and endurance
racing in the mid-1980s.

Like Honda's CB1100R and VF1000R before
it, the RC30 was a homologation special; created as
a limited-edition, money-no-object basis for
competition success. But the gorgeous V4 was
more purposeful even than its predecessors. Its
style and format followed the RVF to an
unprecedented degree, from its compact twin-

headlamp fairing and single seat unit to a
lightweight twin-spar aluminium frame that was
rumoured to be cast from the same dies as the
racer's. It had a single-sided swingarm, as
employed on Honda's endurance racers to speed
wheel changes.

The RC30's liquid-cooled, dohc 90-degree V4
was a tuned and lightened version of the unit from
Honda's VFR750F roadster. It used a 360-degree
crankshaft, like the RVF racers but unlike the 180-
degree 750F, as this gave better drive out of
corners. Conrods were forged from lightweight
titanium. The 16 valves were operated by buckets
and shims instead of tappets.

Larger carburettors, twin curved radiators and a
complex single-muffler exhaust system were
further RFV style features. Maximum output was
112bhp at 11,000rpm, an increase of 7bhp over the
750F. Equally importantly, the RC30 churned out
generous helpings of smooth, free-revving power
from low revs, which combined with the close-ratio
gearbox to make the bike wonderfully easy to ride
very fast indeed.

Droning exhaust note

The Honda's top speed of 155mph (249km/h) was
impressive; equally so was the rapid but
deceptively lazy feeling way in which it
accelerated, with a trademark flat drone from the
360-degree V4's exhaust. Inevitably the engine was
far less happy in town, where its ultra-tall first gear,
good for more than 80mph (129km/h), strained the
clutch and was as impractical as the stretched-out
riding position (not to mention other features
including the small fuel tank, inaccessible tap and
narrow mirrors).

Chassis layout and ergonomics were designed
solely for the track. The screen and handlebars
were low, the footrests high. The all-important
tachometer and temperature gauge were foam-
mounted, while unnecessary parts including the
speedometer were separate for easy removal. The
compact wheelbase and steering geometry matched
the RVF's, and at 407lb (185kg) the RC30 was
light even with all its roadgoing parts fitted.

Cycle parts were of very high quality, with
43mm forks and 310mm diameter front brake discs,
just like the RVF. Front and rear suspension were

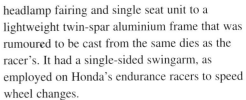

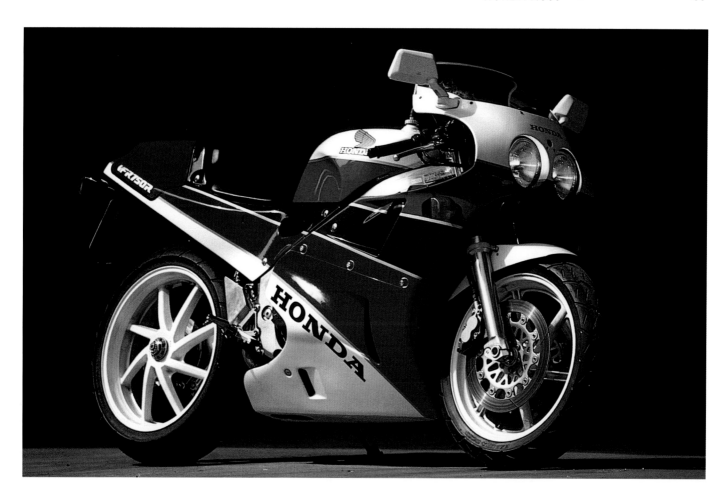

adjustable for compression and rebound damping. Although the single-sided swingarm was slightly heavier than a twin-sider of equal strength (despite Honda's claims to the contrary), it looked sensational and emphasized the RVF heritage.

The RC30 had been built to win races, and it duly delivered. America's Fred Merkel (Superbike) and Britain's Carl Fogarty (Formula One) rode race-kitted RC30s to consecutive world titles in 1988 and '89, against works opposition. Less desirably, in National level production-based racing, there was little chance of winning unless you rode a Honda, which cost almost twice as much as rival 750s.

That soured the RC30's impact for some riders, but those lucky enough to ride one were soon won over. On the right road, just as on a racetrack, the RC30 was supremely rapid and rewarding. Its power and throttle response were magnificent; its agility, suspension control and braking power without equal. The RC30 remained a fine roadster and an outstanding example of Honda's engineering ability, long after its impact on the world's racetracks had faded.

Above: Half-close your eyes and the RC30 could be a factory RVF endurance racer, complete with single-sided swingarm for rapid rear wheel changes.

Left: At its best the RC30's handling was unbeatable but, like the racebike that in many ways it was, the Honda required careful setting-up.

Specification	Honda RC30 (1988)
Engine	Liquid-cooled dohc 16-valve 90-degree V4
Capacity	748cc (70 x 48.6mm)
Maximum power	112bhp @ 11,000rpm
Transmission	Six-speed, chain final drive
Frame	Aluminium twin spar
Suspension	Telescopic front; single shock rear
Brakes	Twin discs front; disc rear
Weight	407lb (185kg) dry
Top speed	155mph (249km/h)

Kawasaki ZZ-R1100

**Top speed
175mph**
282km/h

*Right: Sheer power and
speed were the original
ZZ-R's main claims to fame,
but for a big machine the
Kawasaki went round
corners in style.*

*Below: In 1993 the ZZ-R
was revised with a taller
screen, larger fuel tank and
new frame. Its high-speed
ability remained – following
the press launch in Arizona,
three journalists were jailed
for speeding.*

When Kawasaki's engineers set out to
create the world's fastest bike in the late
1980s, they had the advantage of many
years' experience in designing powerful four-
cylinder engines – plus one very significant
technical innovation. The result was a new
superbike, the ZZ-R1100, whose liquid-cooled,
four-cylinder engine, boosted by a novel 'ram air'
system, produced 145bhp and sent the bike hurtling
to 175mph (282km/h).

That level of performance put the Kawasaki far
ahead of all opposition when it was launched in
1990, and it remained the world's fastest bike for
the next five years. There was much more to the
ZZ-R (known as the ZX-11 in the States) than its
engine, for it was a refined and efficient sports-
tourer. But there was no escaping the fact that the
Kawasaki's trump card was its phenomenal
straight-line speed.

Forced induction, to give the ram air system its
conventional name, was derived from Formula One
racecar technology. It was a sealed system that
ducted air from a slot in the fairing's nose, directly
to the unusually large airbox. The faster the
Kawasaki went, the more cool air was forced
through its carburettors and into the engine.

Intake system apart, the ZZ-R had much in
common with the ZX-10, its predecessor as
Kawasaki's flagship. Bulbous bodywork held
faired-in indicators; the chassis was based on a
rigid twin-spar aluminium frame. The new engine
shared the ZX-10's liquid-cooled, 16-valve layout
but had a 2mm larger bore, increasing capacity to
1052cc. Other changes included larger valves, new

camshafts, lightened pistons, a new curved radiator and a more efficient twin-silencer exhaust system.

When the throttle was wound open above 5000rpm, smooth power sent the bike rocketing forward. It kicked into hyperdrive at around 7000rpm and kept the rider's arms and reflexes stretched as it snarled to the 11,000rpm redline through the efficient six-speed gearbox. In contrast the response below 4000rpm was weak, though an improvement over that of the ZX-10.

High speed composure and stability were remarkable. Even with the scenery and road flashing past at over 150mph (241km/h), the protection of its fairing and the quality of its chassis give the impression of travelling much less rapidly. American magazine *Cycle* managed a genuine 175mph (282km/h) from their full-power ZZ-R1100. Bikes in many European countries left the dealerships slightly slower due to politically enforced power limits. In most cases these were implemented by carburettor restrictors that were easy to remove.

Although the ZZ-R's frame resembled that of the ZX-10 it was slightly thicker and stiffer, as well as 10mm (0.4in) shorter in the wheelbase. Steering geometry was steeper and the cycle parts were also new. Fork legs were enlarged to 43mm in diameter and, like the single rear shock, were adjustable for rebound damping as well as spring preload.

Well-balanced feel

The ZZ-R was a long, roomy bike that was far too heavy to be mistaken for a sports bike, but it handled well. Much of the mass seemed to drop away on the move, and the stiff chassis and firm suspension gave the Kawasaki a well-balanced feel. It was stable even at high speed, and its triple disc brake system was powerful.

This was just as well, because if any bike needed good brakes it was the ZZ-R. The bike's comfort and practicality contributed to its reputation as a fine all-rounder. Numerous neat details included a comfortable seat, clear mirrors, bungee hooks and a much-needed grab-rail. But all those things were insignificant when compared with the ZZ-R1100's greatest asset: the magnificent, ram-air assisted motor that generated its all-conquering speed.

Above: The distinctive ZZ-R shape would remain essentially unchanged through several revisions and more than a decade of development. Key to the 16-valve motor's performance was its ram-air induction system, fed via a slot in the fairing nose. But despite its deserved reputation for speed, the ZZ-R was always more of an all-rounder than a pure performance machine.

Specification	Kawasaki ZZ-R1100 (ZX-11) (1990)
Engine	Liquid-cooled dohc 16-valve four
Capacity	1052cc (76 x 58mm)
Maximum power	145bhp @ 9500rpm
Transmission	Six-speed, chain final drive
Frame	Aluminium twin spar
Suspension	Telescopic front; single shock rear
Brakes	Twin discs front; disc rear
Weight	502lb (228kg) dry
Top speed	175mph (282km/h)

Honda CBR900RR

**Top speed
160mph**
257km/h

Right: The fairing's holes were designed to 'enhance airflow to improve cornering performance', according to Honda. The feature was quietly dropped on later models.

Below: Apart from using a 16-inch front wheel instead of the normal 17-incher, the original Blade's layout was ordinary. Its combination of power and light weight was anything but.

In retrospect, it all seemed so simple. The key to Honda's stunning CBR900RR was that it packed a powerful, open-class four-cylinder engine in a chassis small and light enough to belong to a 600cc middleweight. The result was dynamite. When the bike they named the FireBlade was launched in 1992, it was the hardest-charging, sharpest-handling, shortest-stopping big-bore sports machine ever seen.

Of course, Honda's task had in reality been far from easy. To create such a powerful yet compact and reliable engine was very difficult; to package it in an ultra-light chassis that was both agile and stable even harder. Yet the team led by Tadao Baba succeeded, and in the process created the legend of the FireBlade and began a new era of two-wheeled high performance.

The CBR relied on the conventional technology of a twin-cam, liquid-cooled, 16-valve straight four. The 893cc motor was physically barely larger than Honda's CBR600F engine. It was very light, too,

despite the absence of expensive titanium. There was nothing radical about the design, it was just that nobody before had put together such a refined and compact package that approached the Blade's peak output of 124bhp at 10,500rpm.

The same was true of the chassis, which added a few twists to the familiar twin-spar alloy design to produce a bike whose 407lb (185kg) weight

Erion's Racing RR

The CBR900RR's capacity made it ineligible for World Superbike and many other four-stroke race series, but the Honda was very successful in America. Erion Racing's highly tuned, 170bhp, 180mph (290km/h) RRs won the 1993 AMA endurance title and the following season's Unlimited Team Challenge. In late 1994, team boss Kevin Erion launched a roadgoing replica, incorporating ram air, 918cc capacity, polished engine internals, new cams, Keihin flat-slide carbs, race pipe and 144 rear-wheel horsepower. Numerous chassis modifications reduced weight to 378lb (172kg) and improved handling too. At $35,000, the Erion 900RR Replica was expensive, but very few bikes provided comparable roadgoing performance.

figure belonged in the middleweight class. The thick conventional forks held a 16-inch front wheel; four-piston front brake calipers bit on drilled discs. Steering geometry was remarkable at the time; closer to grand prix racebike figures than to those of the Honda's roadster rivals.

More to the point, the RR performed like a purpose-built racebike too. Engine performance combined instant throttle response, minimal vibration and adequate low-rev power, before the serious urge arrived at 6000rpm. At 9000rpm the RR shifted into hyperdrive, screaming to the 11,000rpm redline with renewed thrust. Top speed was around 160mph (257km/h), slightly down on larger-engined rivals from Suzuki and Yamaha. The smaller engine also lacked a little mid-range by comparison, encouraging frequent use of its six-speed gearbox. But the lightweight Honda was a match for anything on acceleration.

Stunningly light steering

It was in corners that the FireBlade's lack of size and weight made most difference, for no other open-class Japanese sportster provided agility in the same league. Steering was stunningly light and quick, bordering on the nervous yet responding to every command with pinpoint accuracy. The CBR's cornering ability was also partly due to its firm and well-damped suspension.

A combination of efficient fairing, wide seat and generous leg-room made the FireBlade reasonably comfortable. This was no sports-tourer, however, but a brilliant, purpose-built sportster; the

quickest, nimblest superbike ever to come out of Japan. Honda claimed that in developing the FireBlade, they had set out to rewrite the rules of motorcycle design. For once, what sounded like a typical piece of advertising hype rang true.

Below: Compact dimensions, light weight and a taut chassis gave handling that was agile to the point of occasional instability.

Specification	Honda CBR900RR (1992)
Engine	Liquid-cooled dohc 16-valve four
Capacity	893cc (70 x 58mm)
Maximum power	124bhp @ 10,500rpm
Transmission	Six-speed, chain final drive
Frame	Aluminium twin spar
Suspension	Telescopic front; single shock rear
Brakes	Twin discs front; disc rear
Weight	407lb (185kg) dry
Top speed	160mph (257km/h)

Ducati 916

**Top speed
160mph**
257km/h

*Below: Stunning on the
916's launch in 1994, and
still being produced with a
barely changed look well
into the 21st century,
Ducati's eight-valve flagship
proved that high style need
not go out of fashion. The
Italian firm had considered
using an aluminium beam
frame, before opting to
combine a traditional
tubular steel ladder frame
with an eye-catching single-
sided swingarm.*

Rarely has a motorcycle combined style and speed to such devastating effect as Ducati's 916. The Italian V-twin's blend of breathtaking beauty, thunderous engine performance and sublime handling made it an instant hit on the bike's launch in 1994. By the end of the decade, 916-based machines had won a string of World Superbike titles. Meanwhile the roadster went from strength to strength, its engine enlarged but its look proudly intact.

The 916 was a development of the liquid-cooled, eight-valve desmodromic V-twin line that stretched back to the 851 of 1988. More than simply aerodynamic, designer Massimo Tamburini's creation was inspired. The fairing's sharp nose held aggressive twin headlights. Elegant scarlet shapes were everywhere in the fuel tank and fairing. The rear end, with its diminutive tailpiece, high-level silencers and single-sided swingarm, was equally dramatic.

Ducati's 916cc motor was a bored-out version of the unit from the previous 888 model. Other changes included a revised Weber fuel-injection system plus the addition of a larger, curved radiator. Breathing was uprated with a large airbox fed by intakes running back from the fairing nose. In combination with a new exhaust system, this raised the eight-valve motor's peak output by a few horsepower to 114bhp at 9000rpm.

Chassis design combined Ducati's traditional steel ladder frame with a tubular aluminium rear subframe. The 916 differed from the 888 by using a second rear engine mount for extra rigidity. There was nothing traditional about the aluminium swingarm that curved round the huge 190-section rear tyre before swooping back to anchor the three-spoke wheel. Tamburini admitted that this was not the purest engineering solution, but considered the compromise worthwhile for the boost it brought to the bike's high-tech image.

Neat engineering

There was more neat engineering at the steering head, which featured adjustable geometry plus a horizontally mounted steering damper. More conventionally, the swingarm worked a vertical, multi-adjustable Showa shock. The Japanese firm also provided the 43mm upside-down forks, which held a 17-inch front wheel. Braking was by Brembo.

Ducati's eight-valve engine had long been a torquey, charismatic powerplant, and the 916 unit was the best yet. Its mid-range response was majestic, sending the bike rocketing out of corners from as low as 5000rpm to the accompaniment of a spine-tingling exhaust growl. High-rev acceleration was smooth and strong, too, sending the 916 to a top speed of 160mph (257km/h).

Handling was superb, justifying Ducati's decision to stick with a steel frame, after considering a switch to aluminium. At 429lb (195kg) the 916 was light, its frame was rigid, and its suspension of high quality. Although the Ducati was not the quickest-steering of superbikes, it had a confidence-inspiring blend of stability and neutral cornering feel.

This most purposeful of Italian sportsters was not always an easy companion, especially in town, where its racy riding position, firm suspension and snatchy power delivery made life unpleasant. On the right road, though, the 916 was simply magical; one of those rare machines that left all those who rode it stunned by its unmatched combination of beauty, character and performance.

Ducati's Superbike Dominance

The roadgoing 916 was a hit in the showrooms, and Ducati's factory racebike of the same name was even more successful in the World Superbike championship. The red V-twins were the dominant force in the most prestigious four-stroke racing series, notably with Carl Fogarty. The British rider won in 1994 and again a year later. Australian ace Troy Corser retained the crown for Ducati in 1996 before Fogarty, who had left for Honda, returned to regain the title in 1998. His fourth championship, in 1999, made it five in six years for the Italian V-twin.

Left: The 916cc capacity came from enlarging the previous 888cc V-twin engine. Other revisions included the fuel-injection system, a bigger airbox and a new exhaust system.

Below left: Superb handling was a key factor in the 916's success on road and track. Although not the quickest steering of bikes, the Ducati was beautifully balanced and immensely stable.

Specification	Ducati 916 (1994)
Engine	Liquid-cooled dohc eight-valve 90-degree V-twin
Capacity	916cc (94 x 66mm)
Maximum power	114bhp @ 9000rpm
Transmission	Six-speed, chain final drive
Frame	Tubular steel ladder
Suspension	Telescopic front; single shock rear
Brakes	Twin discs front; disc rear
Weight	429lb (195kg) dry
Top speed	160mph (257km/h)

Honda Super Blackbird

**Top speed
180mph**
290km/h

*Below: Aerodynamics
played a key part in the
Blackbird's design, as the
bike's bodywork was shaped
to give minimum frontal
area and a drag coefficient
lower even than that of
Honda's tiny NSR250
sportster. The fairing's
narrow width was achieved
partly thanks to the
innovative 'piggy-back'
headlight with its main
beam unit set above and
behind the dip beam.*

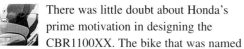

There was little doubt about Honda's prime motivation in designing the CBR1100XX. The bike that was named the Super Blackbird, after the high-speed American spy-plane, was built to recapture the unofficial title of World's Fastest Motorcycle from Kawasaki's ZZ-R1100. The bid was successful, as the Super Blackbird's blend of powerful straight-four engine and aerodynamic bodywork sent it flying to 180mph (290km/h). Better still, in the process, Honda created a fine sports-touring superbike.

If the Blackbird's main aim was outrageous speed, the way it went about it was anything but. Its 1137cc powerplant was a conventional liquid-cooled, dohc 16-valve transverse four. Its only unusual feature – apart from its huge peak output of 162bhp at 10,000rpm – was the use of twin balancer shafts, which made the engine so smooth that it was able to aid chassis rigidity by being solidly mounted in the aluminium twin-spar frame.

Shark-like nose

Aerodynamics was a major part of the CBR's design. The bike's disappointingly ordinary looking bodywork was shaped to give minimum frontal area and an ultra-low drag coefficient. Much of the benefit came from the fairing's shark-like pointed nose, whose narrow width was aided by a piggy-back headlight, with twin lenses set one above the other instead of side-by-side as normal.

If the Blackbird's look was dull, its performance certainly was not. The mighty motor was a real star, generating violent acceleration with a deceptively refined feel. The serious power arrived at about 5000rpm, sending the rev-counter needle flashing round the dial to the 10,800rpm redline. The CBR could not manage the 190mph (306km/h) that Honda implied it could, but it was close – and fast enough for most.

At low revs the Honda was typically docile, too, but the emphasis on top-end performance had resulted in mid-range torque being compromised slightly. Cracking open the throttle at 4000rpm in top gear revealed a rather lazy response, which momentarily hindered overtaking. Shifting down through the reasonably smooth six-speed gearbox was rarely necessary, even so.

Straight-line stability

Predictably the Blackbird was very much at home on fast, open main roads. Its straight-line stability was flawless, steering reasonably light, the overall feel sophisticated and very, very fast. The non-adjustable, 43mm front forks worked well, as did the single rear shock unit. Inevitably the 491lb (223kg) Blackbird was rather heavy and softly sprung for racetrack use, but even on a circuit it acquitted itself well.

Braking incorporated a revised version of Honda's Dual-CBS system, which linked front and rear discs, operating both when either the hand lever or foot pedal was used. The CBR stopped rapidly, and some riders were particularly glad of the linked system in the wet or when carrying a pillion. Others were less convinced. Lever feel was slightly vague, and braking power seemed to fade fractionally after strong initial bite.

Neat details included a clock and fuel gauge on the dashboard (there was no reserve tap), luggage

hooks and a strong grab-rail, plus wide, clear mirrors that neatly incorporated the indicators. Less impressive was the low screen, which directed wind at a tall rider's head, generating some turbulence at normal cruising speeds.

Those criticisms did not prevent the Super Blackbird from being a success, boosted considerably by its status as the fastest thing on two wheels. Honda updated the bike in subsequent years, notably improving low-rev response with fuel-injection, and adding some bolder paint schemes. The arrival of Suzuki's Hayabusa meant that the XX was no longer the world's fastest. But for riders looking for mindblowing speed matched with refinement, stable handling and all-round ability, the Blackbird still had plenty to offer.

Above: A top speed of about 180mph (290km/h) was enough to make the Super Blackbird the world's fastest production motorcycle, but mid-range response was relatively flat until Honda introduced fuel-injection instead of carbs.

Left: Conventional styling contained some clever features. Air intakes high in the side of the fairing fed the carburettors; the holes below the headlight were to cool the engine.

Below left: The Blackbird was by no means ugly, but its rather dull styling was not helped by its paintwork. Alternatives to this grey were black and dark red.

Specification	Honda CBR1100XX (1996)
Engine	Liquid-cooled dohc 16-valve four
Capacity	1137cc (79 x 58mm)
Maximum power	162bhp @ 10,000rpm
Transmission	Six-speed, chain final drive
Frame	Aluminium twin spar
Suspension	Telescopic front; single shock rear
Brakes	Twin discs front; disc rear
Weight	491lb (223kg) dry
Top speed	180mph (290km/h)

Triumph T595 Daytona

**Top speed
165mph**
266km/h

*Below: The Daytona's
aggressive styling,
dominated by its sleek twin-
headlamp fairing, hinted at
the 955cc triple's
performance. Although the
Triumph was not quite as
racy as the most
singleminded of its rivals,
the British firm had finally
produced a purpose-built
sports machine that could
trade punches with the best
in the world.*

The T595 Daytona was the bike with which Triumph came of age as a superbike manufacturer. Fast and fine-handling, the Daytona was the first sports bike from the reborn British firm that was designed to compete head-on with the best from Italy and Japan. And although the Triumph was slightly less racy than some super-sports rivals, its unique blend of style, performance and three-cylinder character made it a big success.

A crucial factor in the Daytona's development was Triumph boss John Bloor's decision to abandon the modular format with which his firm had entered the market in 1991. Modular design involved several different models sharing many components, and had proved a cost-effective way of developing a range of bikes rapidly. But it involved too many compromises for a competitive super-sports machine.

The Daytona changed all that. This time, Triumph's designers had no such handicap in developing a purpose-built triple. The T595 title came from Triumph's factory codename, a factory tradition dating back to the T120 Bonneville and beyond, but the bike was later renamed the Daytona 955i because many people thought the 595 referred to capacity. This was in fact 955cc, as the motor was a bored-out version of the previous Daytona's 885cc liquid-cooled, dohc 12-valve unit.

Inside the motor, new semi-forged pistons held thinner, low-friction rings and moved in new aluminium liners. Lotus Engineering helped tune the motor by improving its breathing with larger valves, new cams and lightened crankshaft. Magnesium engine covers, modified crankcases and a redesigned gearbox and clutch further reduced weight. Other engine-related changes included a new airbox, three-into-one exhaust system and Sagem fuel-injection system.

If the motor was a development of its predecessor, then the chassis of which it formed a stressed member was totally new. In place of the old steel spine was a perimeter frame of twin oval-section aluminium tubes. Styling was a key factor in the chassis design, hence the frame's polished tubes and the single-sided swingarm that enhanced the Daytona's sleek and distinctive look. Suspension was by Showa of Japan, with 45mm forks and a similarly multi-adjustable shock.

Compact and eager to rev

From the rider's seat the Daytona felt notably more compact than previous Triumphs, and it was certainly much faster too. The new motor was smooth and eager to rev. It kicked hard anywhere above 6000rpm to send the triple surging forward and its rev-counter needle flicking towards the 10,500rpm redline. Peak output was 128bhp at 10,200rpm, giving a 15bhp advantage over the previous Daytona Super III. With its rider tucked down behind the fairly low screen the triple was good for over 160mph (257km/h). Only the slightly notchy six-speed gearbox and a noticeable power dip at about 5500rpm marred the impression of a superbly fast and sophisticated sportster.

There were no such complaints about the handling, particularly on the road where the

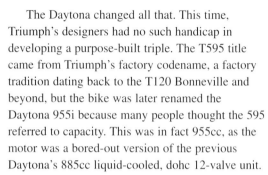

Triumph's combination of light, neutral steering and confidence-inspiring stability was very impressive. The top-heaviness of previous Triumphs was gone, replaced by a pleasantly manageable feel, and backed-up by excellent control from the firm yet compliant suspension. Although the Daytona could not quite match the agility of its raciest rivals, it was not far behind, and its Nissin brake system gave outstanding stopping power.

The T595 Daytona was more than an excellent sports bike, it was proof that Triumph was truly back in the big time. Almost 30 years after Honda's CB750 had arrived to outclass the previous Meriden-based factory's T150 Trident triple and

hasten the demise of the once dominant British motorcycle industry, Triumph once again had a sporting superbike that stood comparison with the very best in the world.

Above: The Daytona's look was enhanced by its frame, made from oval-section aluminium tubes.

Specification	Triumph T595 Daytona (1997)
Engine	Liquid-cooled dohc 12-valve triple
Capacity	955cc (79 x 65mm)
Maximum power	128bhp @ 10,200rpm
Transmission	Six-speed, chain final drive
Frame	Tubular aluminium perimeter
Suspension	Telescopic front; single shock rear
Brakes	Twin discs front; disc rear
Weight	436lb (198kg) dry
Top speed	165mph (266km/h)

Yamaha YZF-R1

**Top speed
170mph**
274km/h

*Right: The view from the
front was dominated by the
R1's aggressively angled
headlights, which perfectly
matched the bike's take-no-
prisoners personality.*

*Below: The Yamaha's
chassis, based on a twin-
spar aluminium frame, set
new handling standards.
The main innovation was
the blend of ultra-short
wheelbase and long
swingarm.*

 Three numbers said it all about the YZF-R1 with which Yamaha stunned the superbike world in 1998. The four-cylinder charger produced 150bhp, weighed just 389lb (176kg) and had an ultra-short wheelbase of 55in (1395mm). That made it the most powerful, lightest and most compact large-capacity sports bike ever built. And with its aggressive styling, the R1 had the looks to match.

Beneath the sharp twin-headlamp fairing, the R1 incorporated some clever engineering. Its basic layout was Yamaha's familiar blend of 20-valve, four-cylinder engine and aluminium twin-beam frame. But the R1 design team, led by Kunihiko Miwa, put the six-speed gearbox higher than normal behind the liquid-cooled cylinders, making the 998cc engine very compact. This in turn allowed the bike to be very short while having a long rear swingarm, as used by grand prix bikes for added stability.

Innovative crankcase design

The R1's new engine also contributed with its innovative one-piece cylinder and crankcase assembly, which was stiffer than the conventional design and allowed the powerplant to be used as a stressed member of the chassis. This meant that the

Left: In 2000, two years after its launch, the R1 was revised with more than 250 detail changes including subtly reshaped bodywork and a titanium silencer. The carburettors, gearbox, front brake and suspension were also modified. Although the changes did not add up to a dramatic revision, Yamaha's assertion that 'the best just got better' rang true.

R1's Deltabox II frame needed to be less strong, which helped explain how the bike could weigh less than most 600cc sportsters.

The R1 engine was a spectacular performer in its own right, never mind its contribution to the handling. The bike felt light, racy and purposeful, with low, narrow handlebars, high footpegs, a firm seat and the smallest of windscreens. And such was the motor's gloriously broad spread of power that the moment its throttle was wound open, the R1 hurtled forward as though fired from a canon.

It was not so much the fearsome acceleration when revved towards its 11,750rpm limit that made the Yamaha so special, nor even its 170mph (274km/h) top speed. Where the R1 engine really scored was in its flexibility, which ensured that smooth, addictively strong acceleration was always available, making it a supremely easy bike to ride very rapidly indeed.

And the R1's handling was equally impressive. The bike's combination of light weight, rigidity, racy dimensions and excellent suspension gave it the feel of a much smaller machine. This was an open-class bike that handled better than any 600cc sportster. The R1 was not infallible, and like many short, light, powerful bikes it shook its head under hard acceleration over a series of bumps. But most of the time the R1 just felt so responsive and controllable that its rider could seemingly do no wrong, despite the bike's sheer speed.

Specification	Yamaha YZF-R1 (1998)
Engine	Liquid-cooled dohc 20-valve four
Capacity	998cc (74 x 58mm)
Maximum power	150bhp @ 10,000rpm
Transmission	Six-speed, chain final drive
Frame	Aluminium twin spar
Suspension	Telescopic front; single shock rear
Brakes	Twin discs front; disc rear
Weight	389lb (176kg) dry
Top speed	170mph (274km/h)

Its front brake was a match for that of any rival, combining fierce power with plenty of feel. Detailing was generally good, notably the instrument console, which combined a digital speedometer and traditional analogue rev-counter with the welcome addition of a clock. Despite that useful touch the R1 was not a bike for everyday use. It was uncomfortable for its rider at slow speed, and hopeless for a pillion at any speed. It was so fast and furious that even some experienced riders found their needs better met by a slightly less focused alternative.

But for those who valued pure performance above all else, the YZF-R1 was simply sensational. Even before it had turned a wheel in anger, those figures for power, weight and wheelbase had made Yamaha's new star the world's best superbike on paper. On road and racetrack alike, it fully lived up to that promise.

Aprilia RSV Mille

**Top speed
170mph**
274km/h

*Right: The RSV's distinctive
and aerodynamic shape
owed much to Aprilia's
grand prix racebikes, and
incorporated a unique
triple-lens headlamp design.*

*Below: The view from the
left reveals the large and
highly rigid aluminium
swingarm which, like the
twin-spar frame, was
designed with the benefit of
Aprilia's long experience in
top-level racing.*

 Aprilia's credentials for building a top-class superbike were impeccable. The firm from Noale in northern Italy had risen rapidly from being a small producer of lightweight bikes to become Europe's second largest motorcycle manufacturer. Along the way, Ivano Beggio's firm had taken on and beaten the Japanese to win a string of world titles in the ultra-competitive 250 and 125cc grand prix classes. So nobody should have been surprised by the speed and all-round ability of the RSV Mille, Aprilia's first big four-stroke.

This was one very purposeful motorcycle. The Mille was intended as the basis for a World Superbike racer, plus a range of V-twin roadsters, and its conservative styling had its origins in Aprilia's wind tunnel. Similarly, the alloy twin-beam frame and twin-sided swingarm were designed by race department engineers not for style, but to give maximum strength for minimum weight. The exhaust system ended in a large silencer on the right side, rather than twin pipes under the seat, because that was the lightest way of achieving the necessary volume.

There was much innovative engineering in the Mille, notably in its 998cc, dohc V-twin powerplant. After considering a Ducati-style 90-degree V-twin, Aprilia decided instead to position their engine's liquid-cooled cylinders at 60 degrees

apart, as this gave a more compact unit. A 60-degree V-twin also produces more vibration, which was cancelled by twin balancer shafts, one in front of the crankshaft plus a smaller shaft inside the rear cylinder head.

Competitive power output

Other notable engine features were the dry sump – more compact than the normal wet sump – and the 'power clutch', designed to prevent the rear wheel lifting under hard braking. In other respects the fuel-injected, eight-valve V-twin engine was unexceptional. Its internal dimensions were almost identical to those of the 90-degree motors from Ducati, Honda and Suzuki. Peak power was a competitive 128bhp at 9250rpm.

The rest of the Mille was conventional but very much state-of-the-art. Suspension comprised 43mm upside-down forks from Showa of Japan, and a rear shock from Sachs. At 416lb (189kg), the Mille was slightly lighter than its Ducati rival but weighed more than the lightest of the Japanese opposition. Neat details included a high-tech instrument panel which, as well as housing a big digital speedometer, could record up to 40 lap times.

The motor was superb: strong at the top end, torquey in the mid-range and with plenty of V-twin character. Revved hard, it zipped towards the 10,000rpm limit through the excellent six-speed gearbox, a racer-style red light flickering on the dashboard to let its rider know when to change up. That top-end rush had not been achieved at the expense of power lower down the scale, either. The Mille responded crisply from low engine speeds

and simply got stronger as the revs rose, heading towards its 170mph (274km/h) top speed.

If the motor was brilliant, the RSV's chassis was just as impressive, combining high speed stability (aided by a steering damper inside the fairing nose) with light, responsive steering. Its typical super-sports geometry, rigid frame and excellent suspension resulted in a bike that could corner with the best. The only slight disappointment was a Brembo front brake that required a firm squeeze of the lever for maximum stopping power.

Some critics complained that the Aprilia lacked a little Italian glamour, but its high-quality engineering and all-round performance more than made up for that. The RSV Mille was a brilliant first effort that fully succeeded in establishing Aprilia as a major league superbike manufacturer. And which, before long, also led to a competitive World Superbike racer and a range of fast and stylish V-twins.

Left: Aprilia surprised many people by setting its 998cc V-twin engine's cylinders at 60 degrees apart. The main advantage of the narrower angle was reduced length. The chief drawback, increased vibration, was addressed by twin balancer shafts.

Below: As well as allowing the engine to be shorter, the Mille unit's dry sump layout ensured that prolonged wheelies did not starve the motor of oil. Given the RSV's tempting blend of instant throttle response and light weight, this was probably just as well.

Specification	Aprilia RSV Mille (1998)
Engine	Liquid-cooled dohc eight-valve 60-degree V-twin
Capacity	998cc (97 x 67.5mm)
Maximum power	128bhp @ 9250rpm
Transmission	Six-speed, chain final drive
Frame	Aluminium twin spar
Suspension	Telescopic front; single shock rear
Brakes	Twin discs front; disc rear
Weight	416lb (189kg) dry
Top speed	170mph (274km/h)

Suzuki Hayabusa

**Top speed
190mph**
306km/h

*Below: The Hayabusa was
far from the world's most
attractive superbike, but it
was almost certainly the
most aerodynamically
efficient. Suzuki's engineers
spent hours in the wind
tunnel fine-tuning not only
its fairing, but also the
mirrors, front mudguard
and seat hump. The GSX's
slippery shape made a vital
contribution to its amazing
straight line speed.*

With its drooping fairing nose, large front
mudguard and bulbous tail section,
Suzuki's Hayabusa was by common
consent one of the least attractive superbikes ever
launched by a major manufacturer. Yet the bike was
a big success, and few riders who bought one had a
bad word to say about its looks. There was a simple
reason for that: the Hayabusa was designed this
way to make it fast – and the result was a
phenomenal top speed of 190mph (306km/h).

Suzuki's objective had been to create the fastest
bike in the world, which meant beating Honda's
Super Blackbird. That they succeeded was due in
no small part to the ugly but aerodynamically
efficient bodywork of the model known as the
GSX1300R. To celebrate, Suzuki named the bike
Hayabusa after an aggressive, fast-flying Japanese
peregrine falcon whose prey just happened to
include blackbirds.

Record-breaking horsepower

Beneath the bodywork the GSX was not especially
hi-tech. Its 1298cc motor was essentially a larger,
revamped version of the twin-cam, 16-valve unit
from Suzuki's GSX-R1100. The new unit had
bigger valves and a reshaped combustion chamber.
A gear-driven counterbalancer allowed it to be
solidly mounted, increasing chassis rigidity. Fuel-
injection and a ram-air system – which forced cool
air into the engine via the slots in the fairing nose –
helped produce 173bhp at 9800rpm, a record for a
production streetbike.

Chassis layout was conventional, with a twin-
beam aluminium frame, upside-down front forks,
and six-piston front brake calipers squeezing large
12.6in (320mm) discs. Other notable features were
the vertically stacked twin headlights, which
allowed the fairing nose to be narrow, and the ultra-
thin, lightweight instrument panel.

The Hayabusa's speed-influenced styling was much criticized, but to Suzuki's credit there was much more to the bike than pure performance. For such a powerful machine it was versatile and easy to ride. At 473lb (215kg) the GSX was reasonably light, and its riding position was roomy and comfortable. Despite having a steering damper to aid stability, its steering was effortless and precise.

Even so, the main impression was one of outrageous power and speed. The big motor delivered instant, supremely strong acceleration throughout the rev range. Whether its tachometer needle was indicating 4000rpm or 9000rpm, the Hayabusa blasted forward like a guided missile. Provided its rider could keep the front wheel on the ground, it stormed through a standing quarter-mile in just ten seconds, reaching 60mph (97km/h) in under three. Even at 150mph (241km/h) there was strong acceleration on tap. The bike was capable of showing more than 200mph (322km/h) on its slightly optimistic speedometer.

All that straight-line performance would have been a liability if the Hayabusa had not handled well, but Suzuki had put as much effort into the chassis as the engine. The frame was very rigid, and suspension at front and rear was excellent, giving a firm ride, yet soaking up most bumps. The brakes were very powerful, the specially developed Bridgestone tyres were grippy, and ground clearance was good. Some riders complained that the low, wind-cheating screen gave inadequate protection. But few had any serious complaints, especially in 2000 when the Hayabusa fought off Kawasaki's ZX-12R to retain its unofficial 'world's fastest bike' title.

Some politicians and bureaucrats were less impressed, however. The following year, in response to a voluntary agreement between the major manufacturers (who were worried about future legal problems), Suzuki fitted the GSX with an electronic device that prevented it from reaching maximum revs in top gear, limiting top speed to 186mph (300km/h). The Hayabusa's wings had been clipped – but its status as the fastest bike on the road looked safe for some time to come.

Above: At high speed the Hayabusa's ram-air system, fed via slots in the fairing nose, provided even more power.

Below left: The view from the front was shaped almost entirely by scientific testing in the wind tunnel.

Specification	Suzuki GSX1300R Hayabusa (1999)
Engine	Liquid-cooled dohc 16-valve four
Capacity	1298cc (81 x 63mm)
Maximum power	173bhp @ 9800rpm
Transmission	Six-speed, chain final drive
Frame	Aluminium twin spar
Suspension	Telescopic front; single shock rear
Brakes	Twin discs front; disc rear
Weight	473lb (215kg) dry
Top speed	190mph (306km/h)

MV Agusta 750 F4

**Top speed
165mph**
266km/h

*Right: The F4's quartet of
high-level silencers gave a
unique rear view. Exhaust
and intake notes were tuned
for rider enjoyment as well
as performance.*

*Below: Indisputably one of
the world's most stylish
superbikes, the F4 echoed
the mighty MVs of the past
with its red and silver paint
scheme and four-cylinder
engine layout.*

If ever there was a bike that epitomized
the Italian love of glamour, speed and all
things mechanical it was the 750 F4 with
which MV Agusta was reborn in 1999. The F4 was
gorgeous and brilliantly engineered, from the tiny
twin headlights in its fairing's nose all the way to
the four cigar-shaped tailpipes that emerged from
beneath its sculpted tailpiece. It had performance,
handling, and a fascinating history. MV Agusta,
one of the world's most famous marques, was back
– in style.

The old MV firm from Gallarate, north of
Milan, had won 17 consecutive 500cc world
championships and built some of the world's fastest
and most exotic roadgoing superbikes before
production ended in the early 1980s. The marque
appeared dead until revived by Cagiva boss
Claudio Castiglioni. After almost a decade of
intermittent development, design genius Massimo
Tamburini completed a bike to rank with the
mighty Ducati 916, his previous creation.

The F4's innovative chassis combined a ladder-
like tubular steel main frame with cast swingarm
pivots. On the limited-edition Serie Oro (Gold
Series) F4, of which only 300 units were built,
these cast parts were made from magnesium instead
of the aluminium used for the mass-produced F4 S.
The forks, especially developed by Japanese
specialist Showa, were of an unprecedented 49mm
diameter. The six-piston brake calipers were

developed with Nissin; the tyres specially created by Pirelli. Tamburini's Cagiva Research Centre (CRC) designed the bodywork, which was made from lightweight carbon-fibre.

Ferrari engineers collaborated in the early design of the F4's 749cc engine, a liquid-cooled, 16-valve inline four that differed from Japanese rivals by having radial valves, which MV's engineers said gave better breathing. The F4 was also the only roadgoing bike to have a racebike-style removable 'cassette' gearbox. Tamburini designed the complex exhaust system after dismantling and studying the exhaust of Castiglioni's Ferrari F40.

Glorious exhaust note

The fuel-injected motor's peak output was 126bhp, so the 750cc F4 did not match open-class superbikes for outright speed. But the bike revved to 13,300rpm, made an improbably glorious exhaust note, and was seriously fast. The four-cylinder unit was smooth and sophisticated, too. It pulled crisply at low revs, and its six-speed gearbox was slick. There was no great step to the power delivery, just a steady increase as the yellow-faced rev-counter's needle swept round the dial and the F4 headed for its top speed of over 160mph (257km/h).

Handling was superb. At 406lb (184kg) dry the Serie Oro was very light. Its short wheelbase and racy steering geometry combined with the top-quality frame and suspension to make the bike wonderfully agile yet also very stable. At high speed in a straight line the bike was unshakeable, yet it could also be snapped into slow turns with the lightest of pressure, and was easy to flick from side to side. The brakes were very powerful, too, needing just a gentle squeeze of the lever to make the bike stop with massive force.

Specification	MV Agusta 750 F4 Serie Oro (1999)
Engine	Liquid-cooled dohc 16-valve four
Capacity	749cc (73.8 x 43.8mm)
Maximum power	126bhp @ 12,500rpm
Transmission	Six-speed, chain final drive
Frame	Tubular steel and cast magnesium
Suspension	Telescopic front; single shock rear
Brakes	Twin discs front; disc rear
Weight	406lb (184kg) dry
Top speed	165mph (266km/h)

For all its stunning looks and innovative technology, some cynics argued that the F4, even the ultra-expensive Serie Oro version, was no lighter or more powerful than Suzuki's much cheaper GSX-R750. But to assess the F4 in such terms was to miss the point – this was a bike that was one of the most stylish and immaculately detailed ever built, as well as one that will be forever remembered as the machine with which one of the great marques made its return. For the all-new F4 to be so beautiful, so fast and so very special was an achievement to match any in the long and glorious history of MV Agusta.

Left: MV Agusta's enviable reputation was forged by the marque's 38 grand prix championships, including 18 in the 500cc class, and by fire-breathing four-cylinder superbikes of the 1970s.

Below left: The first 300 F4s were in exotic Serie Oro specification, with magnesium swingarm, frame castings and wheels, where the mass-produced F4 S used aluminium.

Below: Straight-line performance of the 749cc F4 could not quite match that of open-class sports machines, but the F4's stability and handling poise were exceptional.

Kawasaki ZX-12R

**Top speed
186mph**
300km/h

*Below: With more than
170bhp on tap, a flick of the
throttle in first gear was all
it took to get the ZX-12R's
front wheel lifting. The
Kawasaki's performance
was even more impressive
at high speed due to its
ram-air induction system.
Its intake slot protruded
from the fairing, below the
headlights, to an area of
undisturbed high air
pressure.*

The mean and rapid ZX-12R with which Kawasaki entered the new millennium was a potent reminder that the firm that had made its name with big, four-cylinder superbikes was still a major force. With its rocket-like acceleration and top speed of almost 190mph (307km/h), the ZX-12R challenged Suzuki's Hayabusa for the title of world's fastest superbike. Yet amid confusion regarding its precise power output came reports that the ZX-12R had become the first bike to be affected by the manufacturers' agreement to limit top speed to 186mph (300km/h), for fear of more drastic government-imposed restrictions.

In the real world, away from deserted airstrips and electronic timing lights, such figures mattered little. What was certain was that the ZX-12R, like its main rival, was very, very fast. Equally importantly, it soon became apparent that Kawasaki had not fallen into the trap of concentrating on pure speed to the detriment of all else. The ZX-12R also

worked well at more normal velocities, and was a good looking and technically interesting bike.

Ironically the 1199cc, liquid-cooled engine was not the bike's outstanding feature. The dohc 16-valve unit was essentially an enlarged version of the motor from Kawasaki's 900cc ZX-9R, with fuel-injection instead of carburettors. A ram-air induction system supplied the engine from the duct that stuck out below the twin headlights, helping boost peak output to a heady 176bhp at 11,000rpm.

The most innovative part of the Kawasaki was its monocoque (one-piece) hollow aluminium frame. This was like nothing previously seen on a production motorcycle, although the firm had used something similar on its KR500 grand prix racer in the 1980s. By dispensing with the normal beams running outside the motor, Kawasaki had been able to design a stiff structure that allowed the machine to be narrower, improving aerodynamics. The hollow frame also formed the large airbox. Fuel lived under the seat, lowering the centre of gravity.

Other chassis parts were conventional. However the ZX-12R benefited from the work of engineers from the giant Kawasaki corporation's aircraft division, whose input resulted in the small wings on each side of the fairing. These were not for downforce but to prevent turbulent air off the front wheel from disturbing flow along the bike. Such things were important at the high speeds that the ZX-12R reached with tempting ease.

Violent yet docile

This deceptively ordinary looking bike was capable of tearing from a standstill to 140mph (225km/h) in just ten seconds and a quarter of a mile. Even at that speed the ZX-12R still had plenty of acceleration in hand. Yet this most violent of machines was also very docile. Peak power arrived close to the 11,500rpm redline, but the Kawasaki pulled crisply from 2000rpm. This made for easy town riding, plus effortless travel with minimal use of the six-speed gearbox.

The motor was smooth, too, although annoyingly its main patch of vibration arrived at a common top-gear cruising speed of 80mph (129km/h). Comfort was good in other respects, thanks to a roomy riding position and reasonable wind protection. And the ZX handled well for a bike weighing 462lb (210kg). Its geometry was fairly sporty and its suspension firm. The 12R was a reasonably agile yet stable bike that encouraged spirited cornering, and its six-piston front brake calipers gave plenty of power and feel.

Despite all the speculation before its launch, the ZX-12R proved slightly slower than the Hayabusa in most independent tests. But it was an impressive machine, even so – a stunningly fast, pleasantly flexible, stylish, comfortable and versatile bike that brought Kawasaki's reputation for four-cylinder performance hurtling into the 21st century.

Above left: Straights were the ZX-12R's speciality, but it was very happy in corners too.

Above: The small wing below the fairing logo was to prevent airflow being disturbed by turbulence from the front wheel.

Left: Although shaped for aerodynamics, the ZX-12R was handsome – especially in Kawasaki green.

Specification	Kawasaki ZX-12R (2000)
Engine	Liquid-cooled dohc 16-valve four
Capacity	1199cc (83 x 55.4mm)
Maximum power	176bhp at 11,000rpm
Transmission	Six-speed, chain final drive
Frame	Aluminium monocoque
Suspension	Telescopic front; single shock rear
Brakes	Twin discs front; disc rear
Weight	462lb (210kg) dry
Top speed	186mph (300km/h)

Honda SP-1

**Top speed
165mph**
266km/h

*Below: With its lean and
aggressive look, the SP-1
was a very different
machine to the VTR1000F
roadster from which it was
derived. Low handlebars,
rearset footrests and a racy
seat revealed serious
sporting intent. A seat-pad
could be clipped to the
tailpiece for a pillion, but
this motorcycle was
designed to be ridden
alone – and fast.*

After spending many seasons struggling
to keep up with Ducati in the World
Superbike championship, whose rules
gave twin-cylinder bikes a weight advantage,
Honda finally abandoned its traditional V4 engine
layout to develop a V-twin of its own. The
VTR1000 SP-1, launched in 2000, proved doubly
successful. American ace Colin Edwards rode a
twin to the Superbike world title in its debut
season, and Honda's roadgoing range was enhanced
by the arrival of a superb sports machine.

Despite its powerful, 999cc, 90-degree V-twin
motor, high-quality chassis, race-derived styling
and some neat technical features, the SP-1 was not
a limited-edition machine intended solely as the
basis for Honda's Superbike challenger. The model
known as the RC51 in the United States was built
in large numbers and priced closer to a normal
sports machine than to its exotic V4 predecessor
the RC45.

Honda's line-up already contained a big V-twin,
but the SP-1 shared fewer than ten per cent of
components with the VTR1000F Firestorm. Its
motor differed in having higher compression ratio,
gear instead of chain drive to its cams, and a close-
ratio gearbox. In place of the Firestorm's
carburettors the SP-1 used fuel-injection, fed by an
innovative intake system whose central main duct
ran from a fairing slot between the twin headlights,
through the special aluminium steering head
casting to the airbox, reducing the turbulence
generated by normal intakes. Peak output was
136bhp at 9500rpm.

In contrast to the Firestorm's pivotless frame,
the SP-1 had conventional twin aluminium main
spars. The frame used the engine as a stressed
member, and mounted its rear shock on a large
aluminium lower cross-member. Front forks were
upside-down 43mm units and, like the rear shock,
were multi-adjustable.

Compact and eager to rev

The SP-1 was compact, its clip-ons low, footrests high, and seat thinly padded. The finish was basic by Honda standards, with unlacquered stickers, and wiring visible inside the fairing. Equally racy was the tall first gear, good for 70mph (113km/h). But the motor's flexibility helped make the bike fast and easy to ride. And the engine loved to rev, rocketing towards the 10,000rpm redline with such enthusiasm that the rider's left foot had to flick rapidly through the gearbox, as the bike headed for a top speed of 165mph (266km/h).

The SP-1 was not particularly light, at 431lb (196kg), but it handled very well. Its rigid twin-spar frame combined with high-quality cycle parts to make for precise control. Suspension at both ends was firm, ideal for racetrack or smooth road (though harsh on a bumpy one). And the front brake set-up of large twin discs and four-piston Nissin calipers gave real bite plus just the right amount of feel.

There was no doubt that the SP-1 had been designed primarily for the track, to recapture Honda's reputation for building the world's fastest four-stroke motorcycles. Edwards' title in the bike's first season was vindication of Honda's approach. Equally importantly, in designing the street-legal machine on which the racer was based, Honda had produced an outstanding roadster that blended the firm's traditional sophistication and engineering quality with V-twin feel and character.

Edwards' Superbike Winner

Even Honda could not have expected that its new V-twin would win the coveted World Superbike title in its first year, but Colin Edwards did just that on the Castrol-backed works machine. The Texan's bike produced 180bhp with plenty of mid-range torque, weighed just 356lb (161kg), and proved reliable as well as fast. To add to Honda's delight, a similar SP-1 ridden by Japanese grand prix stars Daijiro Katoh and Tohru Ukawa won the prestigious Eight-hour endurance race at the firm's home circuit of Suzuka.

Left: Firm, well-damped suspension made the SP-1 great for hard cornering on a smooth road or racetrack, but gave a less than comfortable ride the rest of the time.

Below left: Air was fed to the V-twin's fuel-injection system via a slot between the headlights, and through a specially shaped steering head casting.

Specification	Honda VTR1000 SP-1 (RC51) (2000)
Engine	Liquid-cooled dohc eight-valve 90-degree V-twin
Capacity	999cc (100 x 63.6mm)
Maximum power	136bhp @ 9500rpm
Transmission	Six-speed, chain final drive
Frame	Aluminium twin spar
Suspension	Telescopic front; single shock rear
Brakes	Twin discs front; disc rear
Weight	431lb (196kg) dry
Top speed	165mph (266km/h)

Suzuki GSX-R1000

**Top speed
185mph**
298km/h

*Below: The GSX-R1000
was distinguishable from its
lookalike 750 and 600cc
siblings by six-piston front
brake calipers and gold-
coated fork sliders. And, of
course, by the way it tried
to tear its rider's arms off
when the throttle was
opened.*

At the start of the new millennium, many sport bike enthusiasts accepted that the era of dramatic performance increases from production machines was over. After the big gains made by Honda's CBR900RR in 1992 and Yamaha's R1 six years later, they felt it would not be possible for a mass-produced bike to make such a leap again. Then Suzuki's GSX-R1000 burst onto the scene, with a devastating combination of speed and agility that left the opposition reeling and proved that the performance race was by no means over yet.

There was nothing revolutionary about this latest GSX-R, which looked so like its 750 and 600cc siblings that all three were difficult to distinguish at a glance. But there was simply no

other bike on the road that came close to matching the big Suzuki's blend of monstrously powerful engine, razor-sharp handling, fierce braking and light weight.

The GSX-R1000 was the end product of all the research and development expertise that Suzuki had acquired since the original GSX-R750's launch 16 years earlier. Its 998cc engine was essentially a bored and stroked version of the most recent GSX-R750 unit, and shared some parts including much of its cylinder head with the smaller motor. Even the valves and their angles were identical, though the 1000's camshafts gave revised lift and duration.

The bottom-end layout was also similar, although the 1000 had a balancer shaft plus larger bearings. Its clutch and oil cooler were also bigger.

Specification	Suzuki GSX-R1000 (2001)
Engine	Liquid-cooled dohc 16-valve four
Capacity	998cc (73 x 59mm)
Maximum power	161bhp @ 11,000rpm
Transmission	Six-speed, chain final drive
Frame	Aluminium twin spar
Suspension	Telescopic front; single shock rear
Brakes	Twin discs front; disc rear
Weight	375lb (170kg) dry
Top speed	185mph (298km/h)

The four-into-one exhaust system featured downpipes made from lightweight titanium, plus a Yamaha-style exhaust valve for added mid-range performance. Peak output was 161bhp at 11,000rpm, giving the Suzuki a 10bhp advantage over its closest rivals, Honda's FireBlade and Yamaha's R1.

Frame geometry and riding position were unchanged from the 750, but the 1000's aluminium frame beams had slightly thicker outside walls, plus an extra engine mount. Even the fairing was almost identical to the 750's, but the new bike was distinguishable by its gold-finished, titanium nitride-coated upside-down forks and its six-piston front brake calipers. The bigger bike also had a larger, six-inch wide rear wheel and 190-section tyre.

Awe-inspiring performance

From the moment that the GSX-R1000 was unleashed, there was little doubt that the superbike balance of power had shifted again. The engine's performance was awe-inspiring, with a blend of savage top-end power, strong mid-range and precise throttle control that made the Suzuki not only fast but also remarkably easy to ride. There was no step or dip in its power delivery; just massive torque everywhere between 3000rpm and the 12,500rpm redline, accompanied by a vicious snarl from the ram-air fed airbox. In the right conditions the GSX-R was capable of a genuine 185mph (298km/h), and it got there mighty quickly.

And the Suzuki's chassis was every bit as impressive as its engine. At 375lb (170kg) it was only 9lb (4kg) heavier than the GSX-R750, and gained an advantage thanks to superior suspension and brakes. Both front and rear units were very progressive, soaking up small bumps and giving precise feedback, yet also coped superbly with the forces of hard cornering. The six-piston front brake

calipers delivered massive stopping power with good feel and minimal fork dive.

In typical GSX-R fashion, the new bike was unashamedly racy and single-minded. It was uncomfortable at slow speed, and so fast that much of its potential was wasted on the road. That was hardly a fair criticism; a more valid one was that this largest GSX-R, although by no means unattractive, looked rather ordinary. But the bottom line was that for pure performance, the GSX-R1000 was the best standard production bike in the world.

Above left: With its 16-valve four-cylinder engine, aluminium frame and uncompromising attitude, the GSX-R1000 was a worthy successor to the original GSX-R750 that had revolutionized super-sports motorcycling in 1985.

Left: This GSX-R is fitted with the pillion pad instead of the seat cover. Its exhaust is the standard system instead of the aftermarket pipe pictured opposite.

Below: Suzuki's 1993 500cc world champion Kevin Schwantz makes the most of the GSX-R's cornering ability during a GSX-R festival day at Brands Hatch.

Harley-Davidson V-Rod

**Top speed
140mph**
225km/h

*Right: Although the V-Rod
was very much a cruiser, it
handled well enough to
encourage enthusiastic
cornering.*

*Below: With its aluminium
finish, innovative
instrument cluster, kicked-
out front forks and many
clever details, the V-Rod
looked fresh and interesting
from every angle.*

The VRSCA V-Rod that Harley-Davidson
unveiled in mid-2001 was far more than
simply the first of a new family of V-
twins. It was a stunningly stylish, original and
powerful machine that looked like no other
production bike ever built, and which confirmed
that the Milwaukee firm had bold and ambitious
plans for the 21st century.

It was clear at a glance that the V-Rod, long,
low, and seemingly carved from a solid block of
aluminium, was no ordinary motorcycle. Visually it
had more in common with a custom machine than
with a normal production bike, yet mechanically
the V-Rod was even more remarkable. It abandoned
Harley's traditional air-cooled V-twin engine for a
more potent and sophisticated liquid-cooled motor,
based on that of the firm's VR1000 Superbike racer
and developed with the help of Porsche
Engineering in Stuttgart, Germany.

'Revolution' engine

Until the V-Rod, Harleys had relied on pushrods to
open their valves, but the new bike's 1130cc
'Revolution' engine retained the layout of the VR
racer. That meant a 60-degree cylinder angle
(instead of the traditional 45 degrees), and twin
overhead cams opening four valves per cylinder.
Peak power output was 115bhp at 8500rpm, almost
double that of the existing Twin Cam 88 V-twin.

What looked like the fuel tank was a large
airbox, which fed the fuel-injection system via a
downdraft intake. Fuel lived under the seat. The
radiator and oil cooler were hidden by a curvaceous
aluminium shroud that ducted air onto them in a
swirling motion to improve efficiency. The tubular
steel frame was created using a hydroforming
process (involving high-pressure water) to give
smooth curves. A long aluminium swingarm
contributed to the V-Rod's lengthy wheelbase.

One brief burst of V-Rod acceleration
confirmed that this was like no other cruiser from
Milwaukee. The way the silver machine charged
away from a standstill, revving to its 9000rpm
redline through the five-speed gearbox, was
exhilarating. And the motor was also very torquey
and refined. The bike accelerated cleanly from as
low as 2000rpm and 30mph (48km/h) in top gear.
At anything above about 3000rpm it leapt forward

with real enthusiasm towards a top speed of 140mph (225km/h), and simply feeling stronger as the revs rose.

The V-Rod also handled well by cruiser standards. Its frame was strong, and suspension at both ends gave a reasonably firm yet comfortable ride. The bike was stable at speed and steered easily, while other chassis parts showed further evidence of Harley's improvements in recent years. Brakes were powerful, not surprisingly given that the front one comprised a large pair of discs gripped by four-piston calipers. Broad radial tyres gave plenty of grip.

Inevitably the radical V-Rod did not appeal to some traditional Harley riders, but it attracted many more to the marque. This was an outstanding machine that pushed two-wheeled style to new heights, and showed the firm was very serious about combining its traditional strengths with modern technology. A new era had begun at Harley-Davidson. On the evidence of the V-Rod it was going to be just as cool as the old one – and considerably more exciting.

The VR1000 – Harley's Road Racer

Harley based the V-Rod's 'Revolution' engine on the 60-degree, liquid-cooled unit of the VR1000 road racer. Introduced in 1994, the distinctive half-orange, half-black VR was designed to bring Harley glory in the AMA Superbike series, and eventually the world championship. But although Miguel Duhamel scored a second place in its debut season, the VR1000 was never truly competitive. At the V-Rod's launch in June 2001, Harley confirmed the firm's commitment to the VR project – only to announce, shortly afterwards, that the factory was quitting racing at the end of the season.

Specification	Harley-Davidson VRSCA V-Rod (2002)
Engine	Liquid-cooled dohc eight-valve 60-degree V-twin
Capacity	1130cc (100 x 72mm)
Maximum power	115bhp @ 8500rpm
Transmission	Five-speed, belt final drive
Frame	Tubular steel
Suspension	Telescopic front; twin shocks rear
Brakes	Twin discs front; disc rear
Weight	594lb (269kg) dry
Top speed	140mph (225km/h)

Above left: Although the V-Rod's 115bhp output far outstripped that of its previous cruisers, Harley relied on a familiar toothed belt to take drive to the fat rear radial.

Left: Solid disc wheels, a large aluminium radiator shroud and an intricately curved twin-pipe exhaust system give the V-Rod the hand-crafted look of a show-winning custom bike.

Index